THE SECOND AMERICAN REVOLUTION

A  BOOK

THE SECOND

AMERICAN REVOLUTION

Some Personal Observations

JOHN D. ROCKEFELLER 3rd

HARPER & ROW, PUBLISHERS

NEW YORK, EVANSTON, SAN FRANCISCO, LONDON

1817

STANDARD BOOK NUMBER: 06-013587-5

LIBRARY OF CONGRESS CATALOG CARD NUMBER: 72-9759

Designed by Sidney Feinberg

To my Wife, Blanchette,
In appreciation of her patience, understanding, and help

Contents

PART THREE
A Personal View

Acknowledgments

So MANY PEOPLE have been helpful to me in one way or another during the many months I have worked on this manuscript that it would be virtually impossible to name them all. But at the risk of offending some, there are special debts of gratitude I would like to acknowledge.

First, there is my associate John E. Harr, whose assistance from beginning to end has been invaluable. Without him this book would never have been written. During the later stages of the project, we were ably assisted by Richard W. Barrett as a consultant. Another consultant, James B. Shuman, was helpful in earlier stages.

I am greatly indebted to a number of my associates and colleagues who read and criticized the entire manuscript or chapters on subjects within their areas of particular interest or expertise. They include Dana Creel, J. Richardson Dilworth, William Dietel, Donal O'Brien, Howard Bolton, Datus Smith, and Edgar Young. The members of the "youth group," which I describe later in these pages, also made helpful comments on the draft.

As far as "outsiders" are concerned, I have a special intellectual debt to Willis Harmon in regard to several chapters. The incisive comments of Kermit Gordon, Daniel Yankelovich, and William Ruder on a number of chapters were extremely useful. And I have vivid memories of conversations with Carl Rogers and Abraham Maslow.

I should certainly mention those who so cheerfully put up with all of the complicated logistics of drafting and redrafting a manuscript of this kind—Marilyn Van Dyke, Marlene Nagorski, and Marie Gangi.

Finally, the members of my immediate family have all supported me in this effort and have been most patient during the times that my mind has been elsewhere than on family concerns. More than this, my wife Blanchette, my son Jay, and my youngest daughter, Alida, willingly spent time in reading and reacting to the draft manuscript.

To all these and many more I am deeply grateful. But clearly I alone am responsible for what is said in this book.

INTRODUCTION

How I Became Involved

W<small>HEN I FINISHED THIS BOOK</small>, one of the toughest assignments I have ever undertaken, I found myself wondering how I ever got involved in such a major effort. And then it occurred to me that the answer to that question might make a useful introductory note to the reader.

I started out in a somewhat leisurely frame of mind, thinking of doing a book on the subject of philanthropy, the field in which I have spent the last forty-odd years. Philanthropy has been a unique and positive social force in the United States, and yet it is little understood and appreciated. There are many remarkable stories I wanted to tell.

As a result of my years of work in philanthropy, I have had a wide exposure to many of the problems facing our society. This background and two major experiences in recent years led me to take a different approach to this book. I gradually realized that instead of writing about philanthropy itself, I really wanted to examine broadly the subject matter with which much of philanthropy deals—the social problems and currents of change within our society.

A broad approach became more firmly fixed in my mind during the time I was trying to understand the youth movement that was so prominent in the late 1960s. That involvement probably began one day early in 1968 when I had lunch with Lord Caradon, then the British representative to the United Nations. He and I shared a long-standing interest in the world-wide population problem. It has been my major philanthropic interest for many years, and Lord Caradon's diplomatic career had enabled him to be a firsthand observer of overpopulation in different parts of the world.

At that time there was mounting concern as to population growth, but few governments had programs anywhere near commensurate with the magnitude and complexity of the problem they faced. I asked Lord Caradon if he had any thoughts on what could be done.

He said he had no direct answer, but did have an observation that might be relevant. "On the one hand," he said, "there are three underlying problems facing the world—poverty, race, and population. On the other, the idealism and social consciousness of many young people lead them to be very much concerned about these and other problems. And young people are in ferment all over the world. Isn't there some way," he asked, "to relate the two?"

During the period following that conversation, Lord Caradon's point was reinforced in my mind by continuing evidence of the youth ferment, particularly the upheaval at Columbia University. Then I was asked to make the principal address at the annual dinner of the Society for the Family of Man in October of 1968. I accepted and, much to the surprise of my associates, spoke on the "youth revolution."

That was when a broadening experience really began in earnest for me. Aside from being a father, liking young people, and being myself concerned about the problems that seemed to be disturbing them, I had no qualifications or special knowledge for speaking about the "youth revolution." I found that I had to begin at the beginning, talking to many people, young and old, in trying to understand what was happening.

In my speech I said that the youth movement was a positive force in bringing energy and initiative to bear on our massive social problems, in stirring change that will be necessary if we are to resolve them. To that end, what concerned me then, as now, was how to bring together the resources and strengths of the older generation and the energy and commitment of the young.

The speech seemed to be well received. My involvement grew. There were later talks and articles. In an effort to practice what I had preached, I took initiative in creating a "youth task force," a team of experts to develop specific ideas for collaboration between youth and the "establishment" in working on social problems. That team sponsored two opinion surveys of youth and business leaders by Daniel Yankelovich, Inc., which have proved to be extremely useful, not only in our own efforts but in those of others. The task force was succeeded by a "youth project" manned by young people to implement some of the ideas for collaboration.

I soon embarked on another experience which was also broadening, even though it lay within one of my traditional fields of interest. In 1970 I was named chairman of the U.S. Commission on Population Growth and the American Future, which worked for two years to carry out its wide-ranging mandate from the Congress. The makeup of the Commission was representative in regard to age and sex and minority groups, and the freedom of interchange among Commission members and staff was remarkable. We made every effort to hear all points of view through a large-scale program of contract research and frequent hearings in Washington and across the country. This was essential since our terms of reference called for study of the effects of population growth on the economy, government services at all levels, pollution and the environment, education and welfare, population distribution, social trends and mores. The result of this two-year effort was not only tremendously stimulating in terms of better awareness and understanding of our social problems, but it was also a genuine experience in participatory democracy.

In these and other recent experiences, I have come increasingly to see that old patterns are breaking down and new ones developing, that change is necessary, not for its own sake, but if we are to meet our problems, needs, and opportunities with hope and confidence. As time passed, there developed for me impressions and ideas and a sense of direction which I thought exciting and provocative.

I believe that we are at a turning point in our history. Stated simply, my thesis is that instead of being overwhelmed by our problems, we must have faith that they can be resolved, that we can achieve a society in which humanistic values predominate. However, the justification for this faith will depend on Americans generally feeling a sense of responsibility for what happens in their country, on their ability to see and understand the hopeful prospect that lies ahead and to commit themselves to achieving it. This faith and responsibility and commitment should become the substance and the driving force of our Bicentennial in the years ahead. I can think of no more fitting way to commemorate the two-hundredth anniversaries of American independence and the founding of the United States.

Trying to capture and express the learning experience I have gone through is certainly difficult and perhaps risky, particularly when I explore areas about which I previously knew little. But I believe the time has come when the attempt to perceive a sense of direction for our society, to find a pattern and meaning in the currents of change swirling about us, cannot be left only to the experts. Every person must try to understand to the best of his or her ability. For me, this book is another step in my own involvement, and I am sure that my learning experience is far from over.

As I conclude this book, my clearest and strongest impression is a reaffirmation of the power of individual initiative. In the "Family of Man" speech, I urged each of us to become

. . . involved personally and positively in the great drama of our times rather than feeling ourselves to be weary and impotent victims of imponderable forces. The antidote to despair is to be involved. . . .

In my own attempts at understanding and involvement, I have thought long and hard, much more so than when I originally contemplated a leisurely review of a career spent in philanthropy. I have talked to countless people, I have read much more than is my normal habit, I have traveled extensively, and I have listened as I have never listened before. I lay claim to no definitive answers, only to a personal view, to honest questions and honest attempts to think them through.

JOHN D. ROCKEFELLER 3RD

New York City
December 1972

PART ONE

Origins of the Revolution

CHAPTER I

The Currents of Change

Often when I think about the state of our society, a passage from *A Tale of Two Cities* by Charles Dickens comes to mind. It is quite possibly the most arresting and thought-provoking first paragraph of a book ever written:

> It was the best of times, it was the worst of times, it was the age of wisdom, it was the age of foolishness, it was the epoch of belief, it was the epoch of incredulity, it was the season of Light, it was the season of Darkness, it was the spring of hope, it was the winter of despair, we had everything before us, we had nothing before us. . . .

This passage could just as well have been written about our own time as about the French Revolution, for we also live in an era of rapid and accelerating change, of historic transition, the end result of which could be a higher level of human existence—or anarchy and despair.

In the United States today, change is occurring all about us, bewildering, complex, seemingly beyond our ability to influence. Social analyst Alvin Toffler has written graphically about the danger of being overwhelmed by the pace of change, bringing the concept of "future shock" into popular usage.

We all have to come to terms with this phenomenon, and try to develop a sense of perspective about it. Change is specifically a condition of life; the absence of it is a form of death. It is therefore useless and foolish to stubbornly and blindly resist all change. There are many people who take this position, and it can only lead to enormous frustration. On the other hand, those who are addicted to change are equally foolish. In a world in which change threatens to overwhelm us, to initiate it merely for its own sake makes no sense at all.

With change increasingly the order of the day, then our dominant concern must be not how to avoid it, but how to influence it in positive directions. It need not be negative, fearful, disastrous. We need not see ourselves trapped on some runaway locomotive whose speed is increasing and whose destination is unknown. We can do something about the speed and we can influence the destination. We have to face up squarely to the phenomenon of change, try to understand it, sense its full sweep.

In my attempts to understand the realities of today, I have come more and more to accept the view that in the United States we are in the early stages of a revolution—that the currents of change are so profound it is not an exaggeration to regard them as revolutionary in nature.

This view, of course, did not originate with me. So many solid and responsible observers share it that it must be taken seriously even if one does not agree. It came perhaps most prominently into the public consciousness in two books published since 1970. In one, *Without Marx or Jesus,* the French writer Jean-François Revel held that

The revolution of the twentieth century will take place in the United States. It is only there that it can happen. And it has already begun. Whether or not it succeeds in the rest of the world depends on whether or not it succeeds first in America.

And, in the other, *The Greening of America,* Charles Reich wrote that

There is a revolution coming. It will not be like revolutions of the past. . . . It is now spreading with amazing rapidity, and already our laws, institutions, and social structure are changing in consequence.

At the risk of oversimplifying, let me say that I see two very broad sources of revolutionary change in our society. One is people, individually and in groups, who are concerned about justice and freedom and receiving a fair share of the fruits of our society. The other is impersonal and materialistic, stemming from economic growth, new knowledge and technological innovations, international rivalries.

These two sources of change are interrelated in complex ways, at times congruent, at other times in conflict. For example, as I shall discuss in later chapters, it is materialistic advance which makes it possible for people to move beyond a concern for the basic requisites of living to a concern for what living is all about. But it also has created many of the problems which make up the agenda for revolutionary change in the hearts and minds of people.

I have chosen to call the revolution I see emerging the "Second American Revolution," for that anchors it in terms of time and place—here and now. And it indicates the fact that its historical roots lie very much in what happened on this continent two hundred years ago. As for the content of this movement, it seems to me most expressive and accurate to refer to it as a *humanistic* revolution, for it springs from the first source of change mentioned above—the wants and needs and aspirations of people. It embodies a desire to create a person-centered society, to harness the forces of economic and technological change in the service of humanistic values. Its vision is that the ideals and purposes that give life its higher meaning may now finally be within our grasp.

To use the dictionary definition of humanism, this revolution is characterized by a "devotion to human welfare, interest in or concern for man." It is a search for "a doctrine, set of attitudes, or way of life centered upon human interests or values." I believe this is very much in the directions perceived by Revel and Reich. A true revolution, Revel wrote, is a

> social, cultural, moral and even artistic transformation, where the values of the old world are rejected, where relations between social classes are reconsidered, where relations among individuals are modified, where the concept of the family changes, where the value of work, the very goals of existence are reconsidered.

Reich wrote that the revolution

> promises a higher reason, a more human community, and a new and liberated individual. Its ultimate creation will be a new and enduring wholeness and beauty—a renewed relationship of man to himself, to other men, to society, to nature, and to the land.

The word "revolution" is overworked, particularly in the advertising world, but it is important to realize that what is being considered here is revolution in the real sense. There are two relevant meanings—one, profound and far-reaching social change, and the other, the overthrow of one government or ruler and the substitution of another. A genuine revolution can consist of either type, or of both in sequence. It is essential to recognize that political upheaval and violence are not necessary conditions.

By its very definition, a humanistic revolution cannot be violent and destructive; if it becomes violent, it will have lost its course and meaning. Reich's article of faith is that the revolution "will not require violence to succeed, and it cannot be successfully resisted by violence."

Nevertheless, I recognize that revolution in the real sense is a "scare word" to almost everyone, the figurative waving of a red flag. It need not be. But to many it will mean difficult readjustments, unsettled conditions, the erosion of the comfortable and known in favor of the new and unknown. These are real considerations, and one can understand the wish that it would all go away, the view that things are not so bad, that we ought to live and let live. But a movement of the kind now under way cannot be stopped by force or fiat or wish any more than one's command will cause the wind to cease.

Let me say that in trying to understand the forces at play in our society I was not looking for a revolution. The name Rockefeller does not connote a revolutionary, and my life situation has fostered a careful and cautious attitude that verges on conservatism. I am not given to errant causes. I have quite a consistent record as a Republican and a supporter of Republican candidates.

But once one accepts that a revolution of positive potential is emerging, it is time to stop worrying about scare words and to start thinking about what one can do to help ensure that positive outcome. Without a sense of purpose, the explosive forces of change in our society could easily become disintegrative. But a revolution that has a humanistic focus, which is concerned about the quality of life for all people, can provide that sense of purpose. It can give direction to the runaway locomotive of change.

Certainly, the existence of a revolution cannot yet be proved or demonstrated as in a laboratory experiment, largely because it thus far lacks coherence. It is not doctrinaire. There is no tight theory, no iron laws of history in the manner of Karl Marx. This revolution is emerging from the grass roots, from the bottom up instead of from the top down. It is occurring in the hearts and minds of countless thousands of people in a manner befitting an open and democratic system.

Every such broad-based movement must have leadership to give expression and coherence to the will of the people. If we are going to solve our problems, we will need farsighted and dedicated leaders who understand that the existence of a revolution means that we must go beyond conventional problem-solving methods to underlying interrelationships and causes, to a re-examination of our institutions and the systems within which they work.

The symbol for "crisis" in Chinese is made up of two characters whose meanings are "danger" and "opportunity." To me, that precisely describes the present situation. I am basically optimistic. But I also see a difficult and uncertain period ahead, one requiring deep understanding and hard work. The revolution could lose its humanistic character if we tried to repress it rather than support it. The result could be chaos and anarchy, or it could be authoritarianism, either of a despotic mold or the "friendly fascism" described by urban affairs professor Bertram Gross.

My concern is that these negative results not occur, that this revolution be kept nonviolent, that it stay true to its promise, that it not be blunted or distorted or co-opted, but that it be brought through to fulfillment in terms of the improved quality of life for all persons. This book is about the reasons why I feel so keenly as to the promise of what lies ahead. It is about my understanding of the content of the revolution, of what is at stake, of what needs to be done to shape the course of events, of what responses are called for on the part of broad sectors of American society.

It is addressed to the large numbers of men and women of

goodwill in the United States, those who wish only the best for their country, those who ought to see and understand and act. For it is they in the long run who will determine whether these will be the best of times or the worst of times, the spring of hope or the winter of despair.

CHAPTER II

The Second American Revolution

It is purely a coincidence that we are witnessing the emergence of the *second* American Revolution during an era in which we are celebrating the Bicentennial of the *first* American Revolution. Yet it is an interesting coincidence, and a fitting way to celebrate that Bicentennial, for the driving force of today's movement is to fulfill the ideals and promises that were articulated two hundred years ago.

The Declaration of Independence is a radical document. I have heard of high school teachers and college professors who changed the wording of the Declaration slightly to remove the obvious clues to its eighteenth-century origins, and then passed it out to their students and asked them to identify it. The number who thought it was the *Communist Manifesto* was surprising.

The Declaration was, after all, a revolutionary manifesto. It held that "all men are created equal," that they are endowed "with certain unalienable rights," including "life, liberty, and the pursuit of happiness." Its basic message is that when men

10

are oppressed they have the right to take action against that which afflicts them.

A few years after the Declaration was signed, it was followed by the Constitution, which, if less radical, nevertheless anchored the principles of the Revolution. It elaborated the inalienable rights of men and established a governmental system to secure those rights. Here, the basic message is that within the reasonable limits of such a system for the common good every person shall have maximum freedom.

The Second American Revolution—the humanistic revolution—is one of fulfillment, designed to bring finally to fruition in modern times not only the letter, but the full spirit, the intent, of these great documents. To grasp this, it seems to me, is essential to understanding what is going on today.

There is one very specific indication of the linkage between the America of two hundred years ago and that of the present, an indication which has received little attention in the media and among the public generally. I refer to the 1971 White House Conference on Youth which took place in Estes Park, Colorado. These conferences are held every ten years, and planning the 1971 version was a sensitive matter for the Nixon Administration, given the ferment among youth at the time. The organizers of the Conference took care in selecting the one thousand youth delegates so as to achieve a representative sample. All minority groups, all sections of the country, and various educational levels were represented. The result, most observers felt, was a genuine cross-section of American youth.

I stress this representativeness because of the surprising document the Conference produced. There were ten task forces, each analyzing a major topic and making numerous recommendations. But what interested me most was the preamble to the Conference report. The very first sentence said: "We are in the midst of a political, social, and cultural revolution." Citing the coming two hundredth anniversary of American independence and the "high ideals upon which this country was ostensibly founded," it went on to say that these ideals "have never been a reality for all peoples from the beginning to the present day." The goals of the revolution were clearly stated:

> It is time now finally to affirm and implement the rights articulated in the Declaration of Independence and the Constitution. Each individual must be given the full rights of life, liberty, and the pursuit of happiness.

The preamble called for additional rights, and listed shortcomings and grievances in strong language. Then it concluded:

> Out of the rage of love for the unimplemented principles we here assert, we challenge the government and power structures to respond swiftly, actively, and constructively to our proposals. We are motivated not by hatred, but by disappointment over and love for the unfulfilled potential of this Nation.

The preamble is a powerful statement. Many, I am sure, would find some of the rhetoric harsh and overstated, but this overdramatization is only another clue that we are indeed in the midst of a revolution. We have only to recall the anguished outcries of our patriots of two hundred years ago.

These young people are patriotic in the deepest sense of that term. It is no accident that they chose the Declaration of Independence and the Constitution as the philosophical bases for their report. Clearly, they believe in this country and its historic ideals. They are concerned with the substance of patriotism, not the symbols.

Criticisms of "the system" are frequently heard today, but it is obvious that the young people at Estes Park were not denouncing the framework of our democratic political system erected nearly two hundred years ago. Quite the opposite. What is at issue is how our political system functions, how well or how poorly all the many elements and institutions of our society which have grown up in the past two hundred years function.

Democracy is the most fragile and difficult political system ever devised. Its fragility lies precisely in the fact that it is the system best suited to the human condition itself, since it allows maximum freedom for all the whims and emotions, the wants and the needs, of the individual person. Democracy is difficult because men and women are difficult.

Can such a fragile political system survive the revolutionary pressures that now exist? That is a crucial question, and for the present one can answer it affirmatively only on faith. An equally important question is whether our system can survive a failure to deal with the real issues and problems which confront us today.

I am not an unremitting social critic. I find a great deal to praise and to celebrate about this country and its heritage. Yet my purpose now is not to seek out that which can be praised or to work out some balance sheet of good and bad, but to understand the driving force behind the revolution of today. And that requires an examination of what is wrong and what can be made better.

Much of what is wrong has roots in our history, and this is where I believe the young people of Estes Park were quite correct in pointing to the record, to the gap between promise and reality, to the shortcomings we have lived with so long. It is no doubt comforting to think, as many do, that certain stains on our history are over and finished with, but the more deep-seated ones have a way of persisting or of reappearing in modern form. One has only to think of the legacy of slavery and of our treatment of the Indians, or of our tendency to engage in foreign adventures much less glorious than those wars that were necessary to creating and preserving our freedom.

Many of our shortcomings are not the result of anyone's deliberate and evil design, but the unwitting product of some other motive or drive which in itself is praiseworthy. Consider, for example, the pioneering spirit born out of the westward drive to expand to the full limits of this continent. It produced a breed of rugged individuals, but also a pattern of life in which competition predominates over compassion, violence is an ugly undercurrent, and exploitation and destruction of nature's bounty are seen as natural.

Consider, also, our economic system, which is one of the marvels of the modern world and in no small way makes possible the revolution of which I speak. Yet we all know well that our economic system is not an unmixed blessing, that it is exploitive at times of both resources and people, that too few people share in ownership, that along with big government it has produced huge impersonal institutions which can be dehumanizing to the mind and spirit. We know that our system is the prime initiator of a set of attitudes which call for steadily increasing consumption, for more and more, and bigger and bigger.

Consider, too, our native ingenuity and inventiveness, which, harnessed by government and the economy, have produced modern technology. We have come perilously close to allowing technology to be our master rather than our servant. We have used it unstintingly in the service of the "military-industrial complex," as President Eisenhower referred to it, and far too little for social needs. I do not see the current revolution as being *against* technology, but rather as being *for* putting technology in its proper perspective.

There is a long agenda in the area of social justice. We all know that if your skin has some shade of color or if you are of some clearly identifiable ethnic origin, the rules tend to be tougher. It is harder to get a good job, to get a useful education, to live in a decent home and neighborhood, to get adequate medical care, to join a club, to get honest credit, to get insurance, to receive full justice in courts of law.

Much of the substance of the revolution has become obvious in the massive social problems that afflict our society and, indeed, the world today. They are almost all of long standing, but they seem to have burst upon us simultaneously. Only in recent years have pollution and the effects of population growth become widely recognized. It has been two generations since Franklin D. Roosevelt spoke of one-third of a nation ill-fed, ill-clad, and ill-housed. Now it is perhaps one-fifth of a nation, and poverty once again is a burning issue. In the 1950s we discovered civil rights, in the '60s the urban problem, in the '70s the environment.

One could add to the familiar list of problems at great length —drug abuse, crime, transportation systems in disarray, ugliness in our cities (and not just in the slums), weaknesses in our systems of education and medical care, and so on. They may have been long in the making, but the crucial difference now is that we are aware of them all at once, aware to the point that our nerve ends are rubbed raw. We have a crisis of awareness, and this in turn has produced a crisis of faith in terms of the future of our society.

Finally, there is the crucial dimension without which the revolution would have to be called something else—the dimension of values. Underlying everything I have said about the revolution so far is the profound shift taking place in the values by which we order our lives and our society. The humanistic values stated at the founding of our society and the materialistic ones which have predominated throughout our history have often been in conflict. The outcome of the revolution will depend on how that conflict is resolved.

I have touched on only some of what I believe are the key elements of the Second American Revolution. I will deal with many of them in more depth in later chapters, particularly the shift in values, but perhaps enough has been said now to indicate my conviction that we are confronted with large and fundamental and critically important issues. I am reminded of Roosevelt's phrase, "a rendezvous with destiny." This revolution is not one of secret cabals plotting overthrow. Rather, it is wide open and widespread. We can keep it that way and make it work, or suffer the consequences. We have choices to make. This country can become the despair of the world. Or it can fulfill its transcendental mission.

CHAPTER III

The Role of the Blacks

In my view, the Second American Revolution has become a broad-gauged movement touching every level and sector of our society, and will in time affect our national life and the personal lives of all of us in profound ways. But we must not lose sight of the fact that this revolution, like every revolution, had its beginnings in issues of justice and freedom—and the actions of people generated by those issues.

One of the insights in the Declaration of Independence is that people are not moved to revolt by "light and transient causes." Rather, "all experience hath shewn, that mankind are more disposed to suffer, while evils are sufferable, than to right themselves by abolishing the forms to which they are accustomed."

America once again has reached the point where the causes are no longer light and transient and where people are no longer disposed to suffer inequality and deprivation. Men and women have begun to act. They are of two groups: those who feel oppressed and those who sympathize with them.

Unless you belong to one of these two groups, it is hard to believe that America has come to this pass, so powerful are the myths which have sustained us. I do not speak of myths critically, or as if possessing them is some form of weakness. Contemporary anthropology and sociology tell us that every social system has its myths. We cannot stop to rethink our total existence every day. We must have "givens" which are powerful and satisfying enough so that our daily pursuits are not encumbered by deep and fundamental questions. A good many social myths have some historical validity and possess enough truth to be credible.

We Americans have been sustained by the belief that we are invincible, that we have a society in which all people are created equal, that there is full justice and freedom for all, that every person can succeed if he will only try and work hard enough, that we are constantly making progress on all fronts, that as a nation we somehow always end up doing the right thing.

One of the remarkable aspects of human behavior is how people are able to live on more than one level at once. The classic example is the man or woman who attends church on Sunday and then goes out and lies and cheats on Monday. If any pangs of conscience are felt, they will be expiated by going to church again the following Sunday. The studies of small-town democracy several decades ago illustrated this syndrome graphically—how stratified we become around church group and social class and ethnic origin, how we look down on one another and harbor feelings of envy or superiority, and then all come together on the Fourth of July to celebrate the glory and righteousness of America.

Of course the most incredible example of the human capacity to live on several levels is how we could proclaim that all men are created equal and yet tolerate slavery as a legal institution for almost a hundred years.

If we are sustained by the American myths—and we have

been for two hundred years—then it is hard to believe that there really are oppressed people in our society. To the extent that there is awareness, there is a tendency to blame the oppressed: Why don't they do something about their situation?

Sooner or later, every society reaches the agonizing point when its myths begin to wear thin, when the credibility gaps begin to grow unbearably wide. Then the society must change in order to live up to the myths more adequately, or the old myths must be replaced by new ones.

Our myths began to wear thin when the oppressed peoples in our midst started to do something about their situation. I have lived long enough to know that no complex social phenomenon can ever be traced to a single cause. Yet if I were forced to cite one event which more than any other signaled the beginning of the Second American Revolution, I would point to the case of *Oliver Brown* vs. *Board of Education of Topeka, Kansas,* which was decided by the Supreme Court in 1954.

This of course was the famous school desegregation decision, in which the Court, reversing decades of its own precedence, ruled that the doctrine of "separate but equal" was inherently unequal. That decision was hailed or criticized, depending on one's view, as "revolutionary," surely an appropriate use of the term.

It was a fitting beginning of the revolution for several reasons. First is the substance of the issue, the beginnings of overturning the systematic suppression of an entire class in our society. Second, it was fitting because the class involved was black people, whose history and status and aspirations, in Gunnar Myrdal's words, go right to the heart of "the American dilemma." Third, the initiative was taken largely by black people themselves, through the National Association for the Advancement of Colored People (NAACP). And finally, this momentous change was brought about through use of principal elements of our political system—the Supreme Court and the

Fourteenth Amendment to the Constitution—which is totally appropriate to a revolution of fulfillment rather than of overthrow.

That 1954 decision ushered in the dramatic era of the civil rights movement, which fired the imagination not only of blacks all across this nation but also of a whole generation of young whites. In the 1960s the concept of "black power" emerged. We are perhaps still too close to these phenomena to appreciate fully their profound historical significance. More than a century ago, blacks were freed from physical and legal slavery, but in the last two decades they have freed themselves from psychological slavery. The change in the verbs is important: *they have freed themselves.* They are casting off their feelings of inferiority, of low self-esteem, and instead are saying to the world that black is beautiful. And any time that a person insists on his own dignity as a human being, takes pride in his own uniqueness, says that he will not be imposed upon nor taken advantage of any longer, that is indeed a beautiful thing. On the whole, this is happening with dignity and restraint and a faith in American ideals which ought to give all of us great pause for reflection.

It has fallen to this generation of Americans to find out whether people of different races can live together in equality and brotherhood. We must work toward full attainment of this goal not only because we have no other acceptable choice if we are to maintain a democratic system, but simply because it is right.

The road to fulfillment will be very long and very difficult. It may be comforting to think that progress is being made and that in this the disadvantaged person should find satisfaction. But this runs into a hard reality which we have learned only recently in our efforts to aid underdeveloped nations: a little progress only whets the appetite for more progress. Once a person believes that an underprivileged situation is not ordained, not immutable, then expectations grow rapidly, often outdistancing the progress that can possibly be made under the best of circumstances.

The gap between expectations and actual progress has resulted in an outpouring of black anger and frustration, manifested by the chain reaction of urban riots in 1967, by black racism becoming overt, by a new wave of young blacks who find their manhood in outdoing one another in attack and invective.

These manifestations of frustration are not surprising. Progress has been made, but the basic patterns persist—patterns of ghetto living, of unemployment and of underemployment, of inadequate education, of housing segregation. The situation is as explosive as ever. White Americans will have to face realistically such issues as white racism, social and economic patterns which perpetuate discrimination, psychological insecurities which are the root cause of prejudice, a tendency to take decisive action only when spurred by fear or violence.

These issues are extraordinarily difficult and deep-seated. This is brought out nowhere better than in the report of the National Advisory Commission on Civil Disorders (the Kerner Commission), which was established by President Johnson after the 1967 riots. Drawn up by a group of moderate "establishment" character, the report is one of the most impressive ever produced by a national commission. It makes it unmistakably clear that solving the race problem in the United States means solving the urban problem, thoroughly revamping and improving our educational system and our administration of the law, and ending all the vicious circles of discrimination. This will require national commitment and leadership, and, most difficult of all, that white Americans undergo basic attitudinal change.

The report of the Kerner Commission identified white racism as the fundamental cause of the civil disorders. This is a bitter pill for most Americans to swallow. Any discussion of "white racism" and "oppressed peoples" suggests a large burden of guilt for the majority in this society, and guilt is not a healthy basis for building social relationships. I believe that racism is widespread among white Americans, but I also believe that most of us are not consciously and deliberately racist. Too often, however, we ignore conditions and patterns that are in effect racist rather than make the considerable effort required to change them.

Though rarely voiced nowadays, the old stereotypes are still held by too many whites—that blacks are inherently lazy, that few are capable of holding more than menial jobs. Too many whites still cannot see that discrimination lies behind the crime statistics, run-down neighborhoods, drug abuse, welfare rolls. That such factors lead blacks to become more hostile and aggressive toward society in general and whites in particular only gives some whites new cause to be antiblack. The result is a sort of vicious circle or polarization.

A familiar theme among white ethnic Americans is the statement to the effect that "We made it, so why can't they?" On the one hand, this view overestimates the ease with which successive waves of immigrants over the past hundred years have advanced through the strata of our society. On the other hand, it betrays a lack of empathy for the black situation and of understanding of the factors which make it so different from that of immigrants.

In this connection, I was told recently of a conversation between a young black student and a white businessman. The student was making the case that it was black slave labor in the South which had produced the raw materials for Northern mills, giving the United States an edge in the Industrial Revolution which it has never lost. His point was that this society owes a lot to blacks. The businessman's response was "What have you done for us lately?" The young black said, "We've given you back your humanity." The businessman thought this over for a while, and then said: "I'll buy that."

Truly, I think, blacks are helping to give us our humanity, in stimulating and playing a central role in the humanistic revolution, in contributing much of what is native American in our art, music, literature, and speech. Black culture has always been an integral part of the American story, but its impact has been heightened greatly in recent decades as it has become liberated from some of the burden and distortion of stereotypes. The fact is that what has come to be called the "black experience" in America—the tortured history of the racial problem, its scale and difficulty and sensitivity—is a profoundly human experience, one that is totally unique in the world. We are trying to move away from suppression toward a resolution consistent with our ideals, and this, despite all the vicissitudes, is a major factor in giving us our humanity.

The awakening of black consciousness has in turn stimulated other groups to assert their identity and seek equality—Appalachians, Chicanos, Indians. In no small measure, I think, it has helped stir the modern phase of the Women's Liberation movement, and even such movements as "gay power." More surprisingly, it has been a factor in stirring white ethnic groups to take greater pride in their origins.

The black experience in effect has punctured another one of the great American myths—that of the melting pot. At the White House Conference on Youth at Estes Park it became clear that the melting pot is over and finished with, and that ethnic identification has re-emerged. Members of various ethnic groups quickly came together in their own caucuses. This left a sizable number of WASPs who had no caucus to attend. Feeling left out, they gradually coalesced into their own caucus under a "nonethnic" banner. Later someone with a sense of humor changed this designation to "just plain folks." The interesting point is that these caucuses were not dysfunctional. They did not prevent the entire group from coming together at the end to provide unified support for the Conference report, particularly the preamble.

The melting pot myth may have served a purpose in its time, but it no longer does. For black Americans particularly, the idea that you can enter the social process at one end and come out a sanitized and homogenized American at the other simply holds no validity. Each person must find his own identity and take pride in that identity. It is a matter now not merely of tolerating differences among people, but of actively valuing them and enjoying them. Diversity and pluralism are much more valid today than the melting pot.

I see these trends producing effects in the mass of American society which, for the present at least, are paradoxical. I believe that attitudes on race are changing for the better, particularly among young Americans, and that many more people than ever before are trying to do something positive about the situation. On the other hand, one senses a widening pessimism among many white Americans, in some born simply out of fear and misunderstanding, in others out of a concern that the legitimate demands of blacks and the capability of the society to deliver are on a collision course.

The black experience is at once the agony and drama of America. The movement is under way, and it will not stop. Perhaps all one can say now is that the vision of what can be is there, and that change must begin within each person individually. It will help to understand that the driving force of the blacks in this revolution is not to overthrow or destroy the society, but to attain their fair and just share of its fruits. In this, they are in the mainstream of the American experience.

A friend told me of meeting a young black GI on a train in southern Germany back in the early 1950s. In the course of the conversation, my friend asked the young soldier when he would be going home. The soldier looked up in astonishment and said: "What? Go back to that place? You crazy, man?"

It is different now. This is where the action is. You do not solve a problem by avoiding it. We must decide whether this country will move forward toward fulfilling its ideals and its promise.

No one ever expressed that promise better than Martin Luther King, Jr.:

> I say to you today even though we face the difficulties of today and tomorrow, I still have a dream. I have a dream that one day this nation will rise up, live out the true meaning of its creed: We hold these truths to be self-evident, that all men are created equal.

I share that dream. It is a vision not of Utopia, for that can never be. And perhaps fulfillment is to be found not in the happy state itself, but in the knowledge that one is striving to attain it. It is a vision of making it work, of rising above what divides us to what unites us, and finding out in that process that we are all members of the same human family.

CHAPTER IV

The Role of Youth

IF THE HUMANISTIC REVOLUTION began with protest and self-assertion by the blacks, the vanguard of the revolution soon became American youth.

It took the civil rights movement to lure many of the "silent generation" of American youth in the 1950s into activism. Thousands of them hit the "freedom trail," and saw with their own eyes how genuine the problem was and how at odds it was with the American ideals they had been taught at home, in school, in church. They learned new tactics, and they sensed a measure of power and righteousness. All of this set the stage for what was to come.

I remember how surprised I (and almost everyone I talked to) was when the student outbursts on college campuses began to occur. After all, this sort of thing happened only in Latin America, not in the United States. Surprise turned to shock when the Berkeley beginnings spread across the nation, and when we realized that the chief perpetrators were the sons and daughters of white affluent America, not blacks, Indians, Chicanos.

Soon after, there emerged the hippie phenomenon, flower power, the drug culture, rock music, a seeming affinity for sex and distaste for work, and all those bizarre styles of dress and hair which appeared designed to irritate the older generation. Altogether, a learning process was under way for all America, and for many the successive shock waves of the "youth revolution" served as partial immunization against future shock.

The youth movement has generated an enormous commentary, more so over the past decade than any other phenomenon except possibly the Vietnam war. There have been all manner of explanations for it, and reactions ranging from adulation to outrage.

My basic view of the youth movement, as I have observed it over the past four or five years, is strongly positive. To me, it has shown enormous vitality and potentiality for good. I believe our society is far better off in having young persons who are idealistic and concerned rather than apathetic and obedient copies of their elders. There is great significance in the fact that so many young people have shown themselves willing to accept the risks that go with social protest. Their main driving force has been a dedication to the ideals of this society, a concern more for human qualities than for material things, a desire to cut through hypocrisy and inertia.

In taking this view, I believe I am being reasonably analytical, not just sanctifying youth or somehow trying to regain my own youth. I am well aware of the undesirable manifestations of the youth movement. There are the extremists who would like to destroy the society, the dropouts, the drug victims, the alienated, all those whom social scientist Daniel Yankelovich has in mind when he speaks feelingly of the possibility of a "lost generation." Unfortunately, there is always a price to be paid for important social change. So far in our society, it is chiefly young people who are paying it, despite the fear and discontent of older generations.

I am aware, too, that the behavior of youthful activists has often been characterized by naïveté, insensitivity, and their own brand of hypocrisy, as when they clamor to be heard and then shout down a speaker. And yet in my many encounters with young persons I have invariably found that if you are really interested in them, they will not only talk but they will listen as well. I remember vividly when I spoke at Hampshire College in 1970, standing in the pit of an amphitheater facing an audience of several hundred students from five neighboring colleges, during a weekend filled with tension and rumors that I would not be allowed to speak. It was somewhat unnerving at first. But all of us warmed to the occasion. The audience was attentive and courteous while I spoke, the questions afterward forthright, the experience challenging and rewarding to me.

It would be tragic if we let the negative aspects blind us to the central meaning of the youth movement at its best. I see that central meaning to be a desire to achieve a person-centered society, instead of one built around materialism and large impersonal institutions which breed conformity rather than individuality and creativity. It embodies a vision of a society in which each person would have a genuine opportunity for self-liberation and fulfillment, a society in which the Judeo-Christian ideals of love, trust, and human dignity, and the American ideals of equality, freedom, and individual rights, would become truly operative and meaningful for all people.

Far from being some subversive force, the central drive of the youth movement in this country has been squarely in the best American tradition of individual initiative. In the Estes Park spirit of "a rage of love" for American ideals, it is reminiscent of revolutionary America of two hundred years ago.

What is surprising, looking back over the past decade, has

been the power of the youth movement in this country. It has affected a Presidential election, changed universities in important ways, raised the visibility of the environment and population growth as major problem areas, provided the main impetus to the powerful antiwar sentiment, encouraged a more open and positive attitude toward sex, led the way in experimentation with new social forms, sparked the eighteen-year-old vote, provided the backbone for consumerism and public-interest pressure groups, developed and carried forward a whole set of "new values," and acted generally as a goad and conscience to all of us in reflecting on our personal values and those we hold for our society.

Many of these efforts of the youth movement represent unfinished business, and one would probably have to search rather hard to find a youthful activist who would say that very many, if any, problems have been solved.

Various phases of the youth movement have emerged and peaked at various times. We can explain each phase reasonably well after it has peaked, but we find it hard to predict the next. However, it is clear as we move further into the decade of the 1970s that the movement has entered a new phase, a much quieter one with almost no violence and little active radicalism. The more recent efforts at mass demonstration have lacked the strength and vigor of earlier ones. Because of their disappointment that more progress has not been made, many young people have become ambivalent, not certain whether to retreat to a more private life or to try to remain engaged in socially relevant activities.

In fact, some observers believe there is no longer any "movement" at all. For example, Peter Drucker, author and professor of management, is certain that it has all blown over, that young activists have run into the hard reality of job scarcity, and that in the 1970s most young people will submerge everything else beneath the dominant concern of making a career and a living for themselves—just as their fathers did before them.

Obviously, I do not accept this view or I would not be talking about the emergence of the Second American Revolution. It seems to me far more likely that young people have become more sophisticated about the difficulty of achieving social change. They perceive that the shock tactics of the sixties were effective up to a point, but that that point has largely been reached. This learning experience for young people was well expressed by Kingman Brewster, president of Yale University, in his remarks to the incoming freshman class of 1972:

> The demand for relevance, the glorification of the happening, the resort to violence all had one thing in common. They were all short cuts. They were doomed to frustration and letdown, for there are no short cuts to understanding and understanding is essential to true satisfaction and absolutely crucial to real effectiveness.

The time has come not for short cuts, but for long-term, pragmatic, relatively patient efforts to reform. If anything, young people feel even more strongly now than before that the institutions of our society are very much in need of reform. They still see all about them objective evidence of our social problems, and continue to believe that our political system, our economic system, and our social system as they are presently functioning often do more to perpetuate those problems than to solve them. These concerns are evident among young doctors and lawyers, among young social scientists and businessmen. They are evident in the attraction that jobs in politics and government and the private nonprofit sector have for young people. As many of the young are taking jobs and appearing to go "straight," I believe they are carrying their concerns with them, not leaving them behind.

Perhaps even more important, the new and quieter mood of

the young is partly explained by the fact that they now have allies, growing numbers of them. Young people generally do not differ appreciably from their elders in terms of what they consider to be right or wrong, the identification of what constitute our social problems, a belief in the founding ideals of this nation. They have differed primarily in being less willing to compromise, to live by myths and double standards, to accept what exists as ordained. This has proved to be infectious. Ever-growing numbers of other people in our society, older people, are joining the humanistic revolution. The insights and learning experience the youth movement has provided for other people throughout our society may well be its lasting significance.

I have always believed that the response of the older generation to the activism of the young would be crucial. In a 1968 speech I said: "Instead of worrying about how to suppress the youth revolution, we of the older generation should be worrying about how to sustain it." I envisioned that happening in tangible, specific projects in which youth and the "establishment" would collaborate in addressing our social problems. Although this has not happened to the degree that I had hoped, I believe that in a more subtle way the young have made their impact in transmitting their social concern to others.

Certainly, the basis for that impact lies in the way that young people have stimulated many of us to rethink our values—how we relate to one another, how we live our lives, what we consider to be important, how we cope with our social ills. Convictions in these areas are not usually passing fancies. The humanistic values adopted by many young people form a quieter message than all the noise and posturing of the 1960s, and it is a message that will endure and grow.

There can be no question that young people have played an important role in stimulating social awareness generally. But they have also helped us to understand why conventional problem-solving methods are often ineffective. We recognize the problems and try to deal with them one by one. But we have been learning that we must often look beyond the specific problem to the system—be it political or economic or social—which produces it.

The young have also taught us a lesson about affluence. This, of course, was one of the favored explanations of the youth movement itself, which in some cases may have been merited. The view was that youthful activists were spoiled children with no appreciation of the hard work that it takes to get the good things in life, no understanding of what the Depression was all about. They took from their parents, who were probably too permissive in the first place, and never gave in return. But now I believe that the true relationship of affluence to youthful activism is becoming better understood by more and more people in our society. It is that experiencing the fruits of affluence at a young age can tend to remove affluence as an overriding goal. Many young people find it relatively easy to reduce their personal needs, to make do on very little, and they perceive that affluence by itself can be empty. Believing that the provision of basic material necessities is not a serious problem, they are more concerned about the world of ideas and of the spirit. And many older people are beginning to emulate them.

Young people seem to discern, too, that the root cause of prejudice is personal insecurity—the sickness of needing to believe that an entire class or ethnic group in society is inferior before one can feel personally secure. They understand that the causes of poverty are to be found less in the failings of the poverty-stricken than in social imbalances and discrimination. They have learned that powerful institutions and men are not easily moved to change, but must be confronted again and again. They have learned (except for the extremists) that violence is self-defeating, that in the long run its result is retrogression rather than progress, totalitarianism or the law of the jungle rather than Utopia.

The young have brought all these insights and more to the consciousness of many people throughout our society. Most importantly, they have helped to teach us one fundamental lesson: not to be hypnotized by the sanctity of things-as-they-are, but to see more clearly the vision of things-as-they-can-be. The true significance of the youth movement is that it is no longer specifically a youth movement, but a much broader coalition for social change. Whether it will continue to grow, and whether it will stay the course, only time will tell.

CHAPTER V

Values in Conflict

Y OUTH AND THE BLACKS are being joined in the humanistic revolution by progressively larger numbers of people of other ages
and races and groups. What must be done now is to examine the
historical roots of change which have provided the stimulus to
their activism.

Those roots lie in two great events—the first American Revolution and the Industrial Revolution. To a considerable extent,
the values engendered by these two events have been in conflict.

The values declared at the founding of our nation were
humanistic. They were concerned with equality, justice, such
natural rights as "life, liberty, and the pursuit of happiness."
They rested on faith in the goodness, dignity, and rationality of
people generally, and held that governments derived their "just
powers from the consent of the governed." They placed man at
the center, transcending the material and giving expression to
our Judeo-Christian heritage.

In contrast, the value premises of industrialization are not
cast as eternal verities; they have never been proclaimed in a
great document such as the Declaration of Independence. But

they are very real nevertheless, influencing the daily lives of virtually everyone in an industrial society. They are engendered by the characteristics of the industrial state: the competitive factor, the division of labor, the limited-liability corporation, bureaucracy, indefinite economic growth, the use of the scientific method, and technological advance.

The point is not that these characteristics are either "right" or "wrong" by themselves. It is that taken together they produce a set of values, a system, in which humanistic considerations are often subordinated to the goals of scientific, technological, and economic progress. The values derived from the characteristics of the industrial state include: the work ethic, the growth ethic, acquisitive materialism, man asserting dominance over nature, the marketplace as the key standard for assessing worth, a tendency to view labor as a means of production rather than in human terms, a tendency to value profit and property higher than human considerations. The dominant image is that of economic man; the dominant tone is materialistic.

The contrast between the two sets of values might be stated as follows: the founding values are *declared* values, and those of the industrial state are *operative* values. Increasingly over the years we have come to regard the founding values as the *ideal* world and the industrial values as the *real* world.

It is difficult to draw such a contrast without appearing to overdraw it. I am not trying to say that our founding values exist only on paper and never in real life, and that the industrial values dictate our every waking thought and action. I refer to the earlier discussion of man's remarkable ability to live on more than one level at once. Both sets of values have been and are important to us; they are intertwined in our daily lives in complex ways. But the important distinction is that when they come in conflict, as they often do, it is *usually* the values of the industrial state which predominate.

The founding values exist in our society today as the "self-evident truths" that every schoolchild learns about, which we all revere throughout our lives. Ultimate recourse to these great values is possible through the political institutions of our society—the courts, the legislatures, elected officials. However, to resolve an issue dealing with equality or justice or liberty normally takes a great deal of energy and time—fighting a case all the way up to the Supreme Court, for example.

But the values of the industrial state are omnipresent and require no such expenditure of energy and time to be brought into play. They are "built in" to the fabric of modern society. They influence the lives of almost everyone in greater or lesser degree every day—in terms of work, where we live, how we transport ourselves, what we are influenced to consume, the range of choices open to us for the use of our time, how we evaluate other people, how we plan for the future.

Our founding values are frequently blocked by the demands of the industrial state so that freedom of choice is often constrained. The choices we make are governed largely by what we must do if we are to survive and compete successfully in an industrial system.

One might conclude that the conflict between the humanistic and materialistic values is just part of the complexities of life. If it is unavoidable, it simply must be accepted and coped with as well as possible. This is the way it has always been. We have lived in a kind of uneasy compromise between these two sets of values for a long time, and on balance we have not done badly. The industrial state has been very successful. The products of science and industry are fabulous. We have powers undreamed of in the past—to roam through space, to communicate instantaneously throughout the entire world, to obliterate the planet through weapons of mass destruction. The industrial state has brought greater affluence to more people than at any other time in history. And throughout all this materialistic advance we have preserved our founding humanistic values, even though to many citizens they are only marginally available.

My thesis, however, is that we can no longer continue on our present course. We can no longer tolerate two sets of values which are often in conflict, one dominant over the other. The time has come when we must synthesize these values in a coherent ordering of our lives and our futures.

Why can we not continue as before? Why is it necessary now to bring about a transformation of our values? Broadly speaking, there is both a negative and a positive reason.

The negative reason is the strong likelihood that a continuation of present trends will lead our society to disaster, sooner or later. This realization is coming home to more and more people. One has only to think of the cumulative effects of population growth rates, urbanization, environmental damage, accelerating technology, international tension, arms races, and the disparity between the haves and the have-nots. We try to counter these trends by programs of action, to solve the problems on a one-by-one basis. I am not saying that such problem-solving efforts are of no avail and should cease. But I am saying that we will not be able to significantly affect enough of our problems to avert an ultimate disaster without basic change in our approach, particularly in the world of values.

The dilemma is underscored by the fact that the successes of the industrial state underlie many of the most serious social problems of our time. These problems cannot be "solved" under present conditions because their origins lie in the success of those conditions. The relationship of successes to problems can be seen in the following examples:

• Modern science has cut the mortality rate and prolonged the human life span, with the result that we have a population problem.

• We replace manual and routine labor through more and more sophisticated machines and automation, with the result that unemployment grows and increasing numbers of persons simply are not needed under existing conditions.

• We have created large bureaucracies to manage the complex business of production and government, with the result that power becomes more centralized and distant from the people, and alienation and impersonalism grow.

• As efficiency becomes an overriding concern, work is increasingly dehumanized.

• Affluence grows, with a corresponding impact on the environment through greater per-person production of waste and use of energy and water.

• The increasing wealth of industrialized societies results in growing disparity between haves and have-nots, both within those societies and among nations.

• We create ever more sophisticated weapons for national defense, thus increasing the dangers of nuclear or biological destruction.

These undesirable results of industrial and technological progress are almost always unintended and usually unanticipated. We try to counter them by patchwork and stopgap efforts, as for example in welfare and retraining programs for workers whose jobs are made obsolete by automation. Thus far the strength and resiliency of the American economy have enabled us to withstand the effects of the problems its successes have helped to create.

But the argument is persuasive that our problems are fast reaching a critical mass where their cumulative weight is beginning to lead to severe strains and even breakdowns in the system. These can only intensify if we continue on our present course. The end result may well be a total breakdown of the system, or increasing rigidity and control in order to prevent such a breakdown. Either way, the founding values we have preserved so carefully for so long would be lost.

Let me turn now to the positive reason for creating an effective synthesis of our founding values and those of the industrial state. It is that this value transformation will lead us toward a higher level of human existence. Instead of an end in itself, the industrial age is a transitional stage, a step to something else. Now is the time to ask ourselves: What is the next stage? We have matured as an industrial state. Many analysts express this by referring to a "postindustrial" society, meaning a society which has attained industrialization, the built-in capacity to produce everything it needs, and which is now prepared to move forward to the next stage of human and societal development.

The chief purpose of an industrial society is industrial production. The chief purpose of the new society—a humanistic society—will be human growth, the creating of conditions which provide genuine opportunity for each member to develop his full human potential. Instead of having two sets of values in conflict, with the humanistic values subordinated to the materialistic ones, we need to turn the tables: we need to make the humanistic values dominant and operative, at the same time preserving the benefits and successes that industrialism has brought us.

We are fortunate that the challenge to us is not one of turning our backs on our ideals and most cherished values, but rather of removing the blocks to making them fully operative in our lives. If this were not so, if it were necessary to alter the basic humanistic values of our society, then the prospect before us might well be one of violent political revolution, overthrow. The situation would be comparable to those of Czarist Russia and Bourbon France before their respective revolutions. But we have before us a far different prospect—a nonviolent and humanistic revolution, one which has deep roots in our past.

I would like to stress that our task is to synthesize the two sets of values, not simply to turn from one to the other. We cannot succeed by attempting to turn back the clock of the Industrial

Revolution. If the successes of the industrial state serve to create or worsen many of our most difficult social problems, the answer does not lie in undoing the successes. It is a romantic and attractive idea to think of a simpler existence, of a return to a more idyllic state, but for the mass of society that is unrealistic. Revel makes the case very strongly that no revolution can succeed if it results in lowering the standard of living for most people. One of the prime reasons the United States is his candidate for a successful peaceful revolution is precisely our advanced situation in terms of economic, scientific, and technological progress.

In no way do I wish to suggest that the challenge of reordering our values is an easy one, that there can ever be perfect or complete freedom of choice. Our great founding values are abstractions; they become operative only as we apply them to the concrete realities of everyday living. We must reaffirm them, anchor them more securely in our legal system, interpret them broadly, and work unceasingly to make them fully available to all people in our society. We need to apply them to major issues which the founding fathers either chose to ignore or could not foresee—the role of women, the issue of race, urbanization, the distribution of wealth, to name but a few. We need not discard the industrial values, but modify them, make them congruent with our humanistic values, and thereby maximize freedom of choice. We will constantly be breaking new ground, testing new applications, as we work toward a meaningful synthesis. This is why it makes sense to talk of the "new values" even though they are solidly rooted in old values.

CHAPTER VI

The New Values

I BELIEVE IT IS POSSIBLE to discern at least the outlines of the synthesis now beginning to emerge which blends the values of the American Revolution and the Industrial Revolution, the humanistic and the materialistic values as we think of them today.

As I have indicated, the process of rethinking and reordering values was begun chiefly by young people. But what is truly significant is that this process has spread far beyond young people to many more Americans of other ages and in other groups throughout our society.

As have others, I have chosen to refer to the values I see emerging as the "new values." It is the best term available, and it is accurate in that the product of any synthesis is certainly new in an important sense. But the process going on is not simply a matter of adopting "new" values and discarding "old" ones. As the analysis in the last chapter indicates, the roots run deep, spiritually as well as politically and economically. What is new is the reaffirmation of our founding values, the effort to

41

make them truly operative in our society, to synthesize them with the industrial values, and to apply the reordered values to the problems we face today.

We are groping toward a postindustrial humanistic society, and this implies a long-term and complex process of diffusion, not a single dramatic event or series of events. It is a process in which values will emerge and re-emerge, to be tested and re-tested, with clashes, confusion, doubt, rejection, acceptance, culminating eventually in a synthesis—a new value-system as the basis for action and change. This is the most complex form of social change, conditioned by the pace of events, by reform efforts, by pressure, leadership, but in the last analysis conditioned most of all by millions of personal decisions made by millions of individual Americans.

I think it is useful to attempt to describe the values that are emerging. This is difficult because values are not susceptible to precise measurement or easy description. What follows is one man's view of the new values that are important and relevant to our changing situation.

A Positive View of Nature

Man is an integral part of nature. In place of the old concept of a hostile environment which constantly must be subdued and controlled, nature is seen in positive terms as a healthy and beneficial environment. Ironically, the more man attempts to assert total mastery over nature, the more his excesses disrupt the delicate balance of his environment and imperil his own species. Man must abandon his arrogance and seek a balanced and harmonious relationship with nature. This view is, in part, a reaction against the endangering of the environment. It is also stimulated by a reawakening to the wonder and mystery inherent in the forces of nature.

A Positive View of Human Nature

Man is seen as inherently good rather than evil. The task of each individual and of society as a whole is to encourage the emergence of this inherent goodness. To the extent that this is done, the controlling of evil will become less of a need and less of a problem. Correspondingly, there is an emphasis on those human qualities such as love, trust, respect for each person's essential dignity, enjoyment of the variations among individuals rather than insistence on uniformity. It follows, too, that the task of life is to develop one's human capabilities to the maximum extent possible, to work toward mental, spiritual, and aesthetic fulfillment, both for one's own satisfaction and in service to others.

A Sense of Community

A basic need of every human being is to belong, to be part of something larger than himself. One can have a genuine sense of belonging only if one feels needed by others, another basic requirement of human existence. To belong and to be needed is to feel important, to have a basis for self-esteem and inner security. A sense of community is a reaction against the loneliness of much of modern life. It is a groping toward the integrated human being, the whole person, whose spheres of life—family, friends, residence, work—are more related than compartmentalized. New thinking about a sense of community is both nostalgic, looking back to the tribe and the extended family, and experimental in regard to changing social institutions such as marriage and family life.

Individuality

Side by side with a sense of community is a strong emphasis on individuality, on the uniqueness and dignity and worth of every human being. These are not opposing values. There is always a give-and-take, a tension, between community needs and individual needs, but this is rooted in an essential relationship between the two. A good community is one which enables its individual members to develop inner security, an ability to accept their own strengths and weaknesses, and the capacity to be themselves without fear. Conversely, individuals with these characteristics are needed to build such a community.

Freedom

Every person should have maximum freedom to think, act, express himself, shape his own life. The principal limitation is that in so doing he not impair the personal freedom of others. Man should not be constrained on the basis of sex, race, creed, or in regard to his clothing, hair style, manners, speech, or his beliefs and artistic creativity.

Equality

Related to, yet different from, personal freedom is the social value of equality. It does not assert that all persons are genetically equal, but that each should have equal opportunity for self-development, access to justice, and an adequate standard of living. In these respects, there should be no discrimination on the basis of sex, race, ethnic origin, belief, income level, or any other human variation.

Democracy

A functioning democracy is the political and social expression of the values of freedom and equality. It is a social system which embodies these values intrinsically, and thus is seen as the system which is most compatible with the positive aspects of human nature. A truly democratic system is characterized by openness, pluralism, equal opportunity, and maximum personal freedom within reasonable boundaries existing solely for the common good.

Social Responsibility

A functioning democracy is one in which each person, to the limit of his capability, takes responsibility not only for his own actions but for the state of society generally. Unless the individual is prepared to take responsibility, the society will no longer function as a democracy. This value emphasizes a service orientation, helping others, giving of one's self and substance, a concern for the public interest—in contrast to escapism and complacency and narrow self-interest. Such social responsibility becomes the ultimate consideration in the management of the economy and of technology, indeed of all institutions.

Authority and Status in Perspective

There is recognition that authority and status are necessary in many forms for the day-to-day functioning of a social system. But the belief is strong that authority is never endowed in perpetuity nor immune to appeal and due process. It must continually be earned and continually challenged. Authority does not exist for its own sake, but to serve agreed-upon social purposes.

Materialism in Perspective

The value in question here is often overstated or oversimplified. It is not against materialism as such, but for placing materialism in its proper perspective. Supplying the basic material needs of life is seen as vitally important. There is recognition that unless those needs are met to some reasonable degree one cannot strive very effectively for the higher values of life. The value is not antimaterialistic, but against exalting the material to the point that it drives out higher personal values. It is against conspicuous consumption, greed, and excess.

A Positive View of Work

Work is viewed not merely as the price one pays to obtain the material requisites of life, but rather as man's opportunity to think, create, and serve. It follows therefore that work should be fulfilling in human terms, not demeaning. Man is seen not as inherently lazy, but as wanting to be productive. Problems associated with work therefore do not lie in the nature of man, but in the nature of work situations which are not in harmony with human needs. Work should allow for a sense of accomplishment, for expressiveness and self-development, for a sense of relatedness with the individual's other life interests.

A Positive View of Sexuality

There is a relaxed and open attitude toward human sexuality and a discarding of stereotyped masculine and feminine roles. Sex no longer is regarded secretively as if it were some evil urge to be severely repressed, but as a natural, pleasurable form of human expression. In this view, taboos and repressive treatment of sex lead only to stunted development as a human being, while a natural and open attitude leads not to promiscuity but to more genuine human relationships. In human sexuality, as in other areas of life, basing relationships on trust and caring rather than on suspicion has a liberating influence on human emotions.

The Interdependence of Man

Men are seen as having the same basic needs and desires everywhere despite differences in customs, ethnic backgrounds, and beliefs. There is a growing recognition of the mutual dependence of people of all nations on a fragile environment, and their dependence on one another for sustenance and support. Therefore people are seen as fundamentally interdependent. This value emphasizes cooperation and mutual respect among peoples, and de-emphasizes the competitiveness, insularity, and chauvinism which have characterized much old-fashioned nationalism.

A Metaphysical or Religious Consciousness

One of the most striking of the new values is the deep desire to expand knowledge and probe the unknown powers of the human mind, to reach higher levels of consciousness. This often has religious overtones, exhibiting a profound sensitivity to the essential mystery of life and recognizing, at least subconsciously, our ancient spiritual heritage. It is manifested in dozens of ways— in growing interest in Eastern religions, mysticism, extrasensory perception, the occult in general, and in existentialism and other transcendental philosophies. This varied and widespread consciousness is stimulated in part by a reaction against the overemphasis on science and behavioralism, and a growing doubt as to the effectuality of institutionalized religion in guiding and inspiring our daily lives. More importantly, it is a positive orientation toward a moral science, toward expanded self-awareness to accompany an increased social awareness.

Taken all together, these values explain many of the actions and points of view of young people—nonviolent protest, antiwar sentiment, concern for the environment, the testing of established authority, freedom in dress and life styles, emphasis on love, social experimentation, placing people before property. They provide the humanistic base and direction for the revolution that is now under way in our society.

Some people might feel that these values smack too much of permissiveness and freedom, that our real hope is to stem the erosion of such time-honored elements in our society as traditional religion, family ties, unquestioning patriotism, the conventional view of success. I can only answer that such a hope now appears inadequate, that the erosion, however regrettable it may be, is very real.

I think that Kingman Brewster posed the question well when he stated: "At bottom lies the paradox that there is no freedom without order; yet no order is durable unless its citizens feel that their lot is by and large voluntary."

Personally, I believe the discipline and strength to hold our society together and move it forward exist inherently in the new values. I see this in the counterbalancing of such values as "democracy" and "freedom" with a "sense of community" and "social responsibility." I see that discipline and strength in the vision of a humanistic society to strive toward, and in a crucial fact I stressed before—that the new values are solidly based on our best and most cherished ideals.

The description of the values in this chapter reinforces my conviction that the synthesis of the values of the American and Industrial revolutions will be predominantly humanistic in character. We are not going to jettison our industrial and material strengths, which are basic to a humanistic breakthrough on a meaningful scale. But the new values do represent a profoundly moral view—that it is possible through heightened awareness and deep and free human relationships to attain what is good and healthy for man's total being, not merely his physical self. And that it is possible to build a society on that basis.

The new values are, of course, vulnerable to realism and cynicism, to dismissal as ideals that must bend to the hard realities of the world. After all, truth and beauty and goodness have been ideals of man since the beginning of recorded history. But man must survive, he must be practical and deal with the world as it really is. The practical man is disdainful of the perennial idealism of youth. For his part, the idealistic youth sees practicality as merely a form of defensiveness for too many compromises made.

Yet, as I indicated at the beginning of this chapter, the emergence of the "new values" has gone far beyond the point at which they can be dismissed simply as representing the idealism of the young. The process of diffusion is under way, and the "new values" are spreading throughout our society. In determining how far this process will go, and whether in the end it will succeed, the role and response of the moderates—the vast American center—are crucial.

CHAPTER VII

The Crucial Role of the Moderates

A HUMANISTIC REVOLUTION in the United States is not going to be "won" by youth and the blacks. Their primary role has been to initiate it and to provide the pressure for its maintenance. The revolution will succeed only through growing involvement of the moderates—those to whom I referred earlier as the large numbers of men and women of goodwill in the United States, those who wish only the best for their country and their fellow men.

In speaking of the moderates, I mean literally millions of people—those who are now in positions of power and influence and those apt to become so; and, in a larger sense, all those who through their own skill and energy and intelligence are able to work constructively for their communities. The moderates are those who, for the most part, have "made it" in this society, at whatever level of personal competence.

The moderates, of course, represent many attitudes and shades of opinion. Some seem unconcerned about the problems we face today. John Gardner has written graphically of "the 'average' citizens who fatten on the yield of this prosperous society but will not turn a hand or make a sacrifice or risk discomfort to help solve its problems." Others are fearful, and they try to withdraw and shut out what is going on in the society at large. Many are concerned and motivated, but feel alone and powerless, uncertain about what direction to take.

It might seem odd or contradictory to think of such a diverse group of "moderates" as the key to a "revolution," but it is nevertheless true in the present case. The value synthesis I spoke of earlier can be achieved only if the moderates ultimately come to adopt and live out the new values. In the last analysis, only they can give authenticity and legitimacy to the Second American Revolution. Their active participation is the only way to assure that the profound currents of change today will increasingly be humanistic in nature and will remain non-violent. Without that participation the arena of social change will be left chiefly to the extremists of the left and right, and the chances will be greatly increased that the future of America will not be a desirable one.

The Protestant theologian, Harvey Cox, has written of three basic views of history. Like Cox, I reject the first two: the apocalyptic view, that humanity is doomed, and the Messianic view, that it is destined to a glorious future. The third Cox terms the "prophetic" view, which he identifies with the prophets of the Old and New Testaments. It is a conditional view, that history is shaped by our choices and actions: *"If* we do this, *then* this will happen." History is not predetermined by some random pattern or unknown force. *It will be determined by us.*

Our best hope for the future is that the moderates increasingly will realize that they must take the initiative rather than dissipate their influence through reactions of withdrawal or fear or complacency. I believe this is beginning to happen to a significant and encouraging degree. Many moderates are finding ways to effect needed social change—simply by taking personal initiative and becoming involved, by joining with others for a concerted effort. Increasingly, they are coming to understand what young people and the blacks have been saying. They are learning that in the long run personal security is not to be found in narrow privilege, but in joining in an open and expansive effort to create a better society for all. They are rediscovering their commitment to democratic ideals and processes. And they are beginning to respond to the challenge which was perhaps best expressed by President Kennedy: "Ask not what your country can do for you; ask what you can do for your country."

A major pattern of involvement of the moderates in the humanistic revolution has become discernible. It is basically the same pattern that prevailed in the American Revolution of two hundred years ago. The process begins with the espousal of some idea or cause or grievance by persons who are seen as radicals. To get attention, the radicals often engage in shock tactics, and come to be regarded as a menace for having stirred the calm waters unnecessarily. If the idea or cause of grievance is spurious or truly deviant, it flickers and dies out after a while. But if it has objective truth, the ring of genuineness and "rightness" as a social issue, the role of the moderates begins. After a possibly negative initial reaction, the moderates reconsider, gradually becoming involved and exerting a moderating influence. In time their larger numbers and moderate point of view begin to endow the cause with an aura of legitimacy. The process rarely operates along a straight and easy path. Often there is one step backward for every two forward, latent phases and active phases, doubt and hesitancy. But in the long run the moderates may well accomplish what the radicals can never accomplish alone—that is, legitimize the change and make it widespread and effective.

In a general way, I believe this pattern of radical beginnings followed by a moderating influence has been quite evident in the roles that youth and the blacks have played in the human-istic revolution. There are four other examples in specific areas of change in recent years which seem to me especially sig-nificant.

1. *Women's Liberation:* Probably no other movement in our time has had such bizarre beginnings. For a while it was treated as a joke by male chauvinists, and indeed by many, probably most, women. But amid all the exaggerations and sloganeering, some genuine issues of social justice began to become more and more clear. They include the overwhelming dominance of men in public and corporate affairs, unequal pay for equal work, the stereotyped sex roles, the denial of a woman's right to make the decisions affecting her own life and body, the way the English language conspires to place women in a subordinate position.

Millions of women all across the country who would never have dreamed of being out on picket lines, who initially re-jected the idea of Women's Liberation, have come in to exert a moderating influence. They have been touched and they have responded. For most women, the change may not be a radical one in their own lives, but it is fundamentally important never-theless. They are beginning to see themselves and the world in a new perspective, and neither they nor the world will ever be quite the same. And as for men, they increasingly are coming to take the only sensible view—to see that Women's Liberation is men's liberation, and that together they can become human liberation.

2. *Consumerism:* This, too, had its "radical" beginnings, in the person of Ralph Nader and his 1965 book, *Unsafe at Any Speed.* For Nader was definitely seen as a radical, an upstart, who dared to take on one of the nation's most powerful corpo-rations and challenge the established way of doing business. There were very serious efforts to discredit him. But to use an automotive metaphor, they backfired, for they were based on a complete miscalculation of the public mood. Instead of being

some errant Don Quixote tilting at windmills, Nader was the forerunner of a powerful and pent-up sentiment felt by millions of moderates all across the country.

Despite the existence of state and Federal regulatory agencies, past efforts to protect the consumer came to be seen as grossly inadequate. In the face of organized business and labor and government, consumers were unorganized. But now a mass movement has been launched which in an interesting way is an echo of the first American Revolution. That revolution was against entrenched political power, springing from the desire of the American colonists to have a just and reasonable influence over the political decisions that affected their lives. To a considerable degree, today's revolution is directed at entrenched economic power, spurred by those who want to have the same influence over the economic decisions that affect their lives.

3. *The Environmentalists:* The growth of concern for the environment parallels the consumerism movement in some respects. It was greatly influenced by a single writer and a single book—the late Rachel Carson and *Silent Spring*. She, too, was seen as a radical, and there were efforts to discredit and deride her. But these efforts were also misguided, for Rachel Carson was another forerunner of an important social movement. Her cause was picked up by "radical" youth, and subsequently has been embraced by millions of moderates all across the country.

There were, of course, many antecedents to Rachel Carson in the work of conservationists since the early part of this century. But they had been fighting a losing battle. It took unconventional channels to bring the message home to the American people, and we now have the prospect of turning the tide against the devastation wreaked by man upon his natural environment. The battle has been joined in earnest against ugliness in the cities, strip-mining, deforestation, the use of nonrecyclable packaging, air and water and noise pollution. It is far too early to say that no important decisions are made without consideration of their impact on the environment: but they will become increasingly rare.

4. *The Democratic Party:* I have already mentioned my Republican background, so I trust the following remarks will be taken in the nonpartisan and objective spirit in which they are intended. It seems to me that any objective person will have to agree that the Democratic Party has undergone a remarkable transformation since the shambles of its 1968 Convention in Chicago. Many of the dissenters on the streets in Chicago were in the Miami Convention Hall as delegates in 1972 or were represented there. Youth, women, blacks, and other minority groups were all there in substantial numbers. More than 80 percent had never been delegates before.

There was nothing about the 1972 Democratic Party Convention which suggests perfection: some reforms went too far, others not far enough; there was plenty of conflict; there were hurt and disgust on the part of the old "pros" of the party, and many of the new participants ended up by acting like old pros. But an important process was started which fits into the basic pattern I have been discussing. It transcended the question of victory or defeat at the polls in November, for the Democratic Party will never be the same. And it is self-evident that this sort of fundamental change in one of our two major political parties affects many millions of people in our society.

All four of these examples have the same basic similarity of radical beginnings followed by a moderating influence. All four illustrate how very large numbers of moderates became involved and played a crucial role, bringing fundamental social change into the mainstream of our national life. And all four are part of the humanistic revolution, each manifesting in important ways the new values.

In the years ahead we are likely to witness similar cases of radicals proposing changes which are ultimately adopted and moderated by growing numbers of participants. It is also pos-

sible that the beginnings will be initiated less by the radicals
and more by the moderates. Perhaps enough has already happened that we may well be witnessing the emergence of a broad
coalition of moderates for responsible and needed social change,
moderates who will now take the initiative in other areas of
change without need for shock tactics.

Doubtless the moderates who have become involved in the
examples I have cited are those who were predisposed to involvement, those who were especially concerned about the state
of our society and were looking for ways to begin making their
influence felt. There are, of course, many more moderates who
are not yet involved. Most of them, I am convinced, can be
reached and will be stirred as time passes. I have no tangible
proof of this, just my own sense that in a personal and low-key
way the attitudes and values of a great many people are slowly
shifting. One sees this in the changing views of the older and
younger generations in very recent years. There is a growing
spirit of moderation in the air, a backing away from rigid positions once held. Both sides—those eager for basic change and
those resistant to it—have done well in isolating the extremists
among them. Both seem more aware of their own weaknesses,
less sure of having all the answers.

It seems to me that "establishment" members in business,
government, and education recognize more fully than ever
before that the successes of our present system are being over-
taken by its failures, that something is basically wrong, that we
need fresh thinking, that to be responsive to the challenge of
change is not to lose one's psychological security but to gain it. I
believe that young people, too, are more acutely aware that the
remarkable effect of their critique of society has not always been
matched by sustained programs of action on their part, that
their movement has been subject to spasmodic ups and downs,
that it has produced its own pathologies.

After their own experiences of trial and error, many young

people have come to appreciate more fully some of the beliefs most strongly held by older people: that in the long run the ends of justice are served better by conditions of order than of disorder, that it takes hard and persistent work to accomplish anything worthwhile, that structure and organization and some gradations of authority are usually necessary to the accomplishment of difficult tasks, that compromise and accommodation are essential to a democratic order, that perfection is an illusion, and that human motivations are never simple or entirely predictable.

For their part, older people in growing numbers are finding great attraction in many of the new values. Many are beginning to experience a new ease in human relations, finding the rewards in being open rather than secretive, trusting rather than suspicious. Many people well into their careers are beginning to see and understand how their natural human emotions have been blunted by rigid organizational forms, social conventions, and overconcern for material security. Messages are beginning to get through—about war, population, the environment, materialism, freedom of choice.

The rethinking of attitudes and values obviously is the precondition to growing involvement by the moderates. It can be reinforced by the exchange of ideas and through dialogue. But ultimately everything depends on whether it is followed by actual involvement—working together, beginning with small beginnings, and at the same time not being afraid to tackle the large issues as well. No one can say with authority how far this process has gone and how far it will go. I can only say with certainty that the crucial role of the moderates begins with the personal decision to become involved in the humanistic revolution, to play a part in the great drama of our time. And only they can make that revolution succeed.

It is not an easy matter to become involved. It is tempting to wait and see, to maintain a distance for the time being, to avoid the risks inherent in taking a position on any of the complex issues at stake. But this seems to me to be a time above all when every person must open his mind to new ideas as much as he can, think about where he stands, come to his own conclusions, and then try to do something about them.

PART TWO

Some Critical Areas

CHAPTER VIII

The Underlying Challenge

CRITICAL AREAS OF CHANGE lie ahead in the unfolding of the humanistic revolution. The challenge that I believe underlies all others is that of finding effective ways to deal with the problems of population growth and environmental damage.

In my mind, these two problem areas are in reality two sides of the same coin. Together they profoundly influence the total environment of human existence. If we are able to meet the challenge they pose, a life of quality will be increasingly possible for all people. If we are not, the future will be increasingly bleak for our society and the world—no matter how competently we deal with the many other problems that confront us.

To put this challenge another way: Population growth and environmental deterioration function as intensifiers of many other problems, such as urban decay, housing, transportation, crime, education. Meeting the population-pollution challenge will not by itself solve these problems and will not be a substitute for effective social and economic planning and action. But meeting that challenge *is an essential condition* to solving these other difficult problems.

The fundamental nature of the population-pollution challenge is captured by a metaphor increasingly used of late—that of "Spaceship Earth." Like a man-made spaceship, the Earth is self-contained, self-supporting, and has two critical limitations: It is limited in the number of people it can support, and it can tolerate only a limited amount of abuse of its life-support systems—air, water, and soil.

I have always tried to avoid scare tactics in any efforts I have made to motivate people. However, today it is a matter of simple realism to recognize that for the first time in all of history the human race has the capacity to render its planet uninhabitable. The fast way is by nuclear war. The slow way is by the combined effects of unchecked population growth and accelerating environmental deterioration.

In keeping with the basic purpose of this book, I discuss the population and pollution problems here from the perspective of their impact upon the United States. In so doing, I am of course aware that these problems and others dealt with later have the most profound global implications. Obviously, it is important for the United States—indeed, for any nation—to begin to cope with these broad problems on the home front, not only for its own internal welfare, but to better equip it to play a constructive role internationally.

My interest in population dates back to the 1930s. In recent years my conviction has grown that no problem is more fundamental in long-range terms. Americans have been accustomed to thinking of population growth as a problem in other countries, not at home. It was not until four or five years ago, when the issue of pollution moved to the center of the stage, that population became recognized as a problem in America as well. We increasingly became aware of the fact that numbers of people have a direct bearing on pollution and depletion of resources.

To me, one of the most gratifying results of this awareness was President Nixon's message to Congress on population in July of 1969. In it he said, "One of the most serious challenges to human destiny in the last third of this century will be the growth of the population. Whether man's response to that challenge will be a cause for pride or for despair in the year 2000 will depend very much on what we do today."

The President recommended establishment of a commission to study the impact of the growth of population upon the nation. Congress created such a body in March 1970 and called it the Commission on Population Growth and the American Future. I was named chairman. Let me mention a few highlights of our findings, which were released in the spring of 1972:

1. Population growth in this century should be regarded neither as a crisis nor with complacency. While the American birth rate has been declining, there is no assurance as to its future course. If families in the United States have only two children on the average and immigration continues at current levels, our population would grow to 271 million by the year 2000. If, however, families should average three children, the population would reach 322 million by that time. One hundred years from now the two-child family would result in a population of 350 million people, whereas the three-child family would produce a total of nearly a billion.

2. Population growth has a pervasive impact on every major facet of our lives, and important implications for the quality of life. The time has come for the United States to welcome and plan for a stabilized population.

3. In the long run no substantial benefit will result from further growth of the nation's population. Rather, population growth of the current magnitude has aggravated many of the

nation's problems and made their solution more difficult. Gradual stabilization of our population would contribute significantly to the nation's ability to solve its problems. It would also enable our society to shift its focus increasingly from quantity to quality; to assign higher priorities to what gives human life special meaning and value.

4. Finally, the Commission came to the conclusion, based on its research, that our nation has nothing to fear from a gradual approach to population stabilization. It pointed out that it had looked for but had not found any convincing economic argument for continued population growth. The health of the country does not depend on it, nor does the vitality of business or the welfare of the average person. In fact, a reduction in the rate of population growth would bring important economic benefits to all citizens, especially if the nation developed policies to take advantage of the opportunities for social and economic improvement that slower population growth would provide.

In receiving the Commission's report in May of 1972, President Nixon said he disagreed with recommendations concerning the availability of "family planning services and devices" to minors and concerning abortion, which he said he considered "an unacceptable form of population control." Actually, the report recommended that "abortion not be considered a primary means of fertility control," maintaining that the issue is a woman's right to determine her own fertility, and that the matter of abortion should be left to the conscience of the individual concerned in consultation with her physician.

Aside from these two points, the President was supportive of the report. He said: "The findings and conclusions of the Commission should be of great value in assisting governments at all levels to formulate policy." At this writing the recommendations are receiving serious and high-level review in Washington.

Throughout its deliberations the overriding goal of the Commission was the enrichment of human life, not its restriction.

We were aware that there has been much talk and concern about controls and coercion in the population field. The whole thrust of our effort was, however, the attainment of social goals through voluntary action to be determined by the individual in his own best interest.

The Commission recognized that such voluntary action would be meaningful only if there was freedom of choice. We realized that this becomes a reality only if society provides the conditions to make it viable. This we came to call *true* freedom of choice. For example, we like to think that all parents in this country can freely decide the number of their children. The facts are, however, that knowledge in regard to family planning and supportive services is still not available to millions of Americans. Then there is the situation facing many American women in regard to marriage and a family. What is their alternative if they prefer not to marry or to have children? Society often does not make possible career alternatives which will give genuine satisfaction; hence, they do not have true freedom of choice.

I personally have always looked at the population problem in terms of the human factors involved—a concern for the enrichment of life and a stress on voluntary action. To me, the basic objective has always been to make it possible for all people to live in dignity and to have a better chance of attaining their full potential.

The same humanistic considerations apply equally to the other facet of the fundamental challenge now facing us— namely, the accelerating depletion of natural resources and the pollution of air, water, and soil. These, of course, are physical matters, but abuse of them quickly becomes a threat to humanistic values and, ultimately, to human life itself. Consider, for example, what strip-mining, deforestation, urban blight, dying lakes and rivers, and smog are doing to just one of the great humanistic values, that of beauty. It seems abundantly clear that the pace at which we are fouling our nest threatens to lower the quality of life for everyone.

We are fortunate that the threat of environmental deterioration is now widely recognized throughout our society. It has stimulated a great deal of citizen activity—from the housewife who saves newspapers, tin cans, and bottles for recycling to the businessman who installs antipollution devices in his factory or converts to manufacturing biodegradable products. There are now many public-service groups putting pressure on industries and local governments to curb their pollution. We have new legislation at the Federal and state levels establishing standards and administrative machinery for controlling such polluting factors as automobile emissions and inadequate sewage disposal.

We of course have a long way to go. In the following paragraphs I mention several areas in which we clearly need more study and action:

• Because of its large population, affluence, and high economic productivity, the United States is a vast consumer of natural resources. In the case of some minerals and foods, for example, we account for well over half of the entire world's consumption. Experts disagree as to when this or that resource will be used up, but in general the awareness is growing that resources are not unlimited. Unless we cut down on unnecessary and extravagant consumption, the future of "Spaceship Earth" will be in serious doubt. Because our society is by far the greatest consumer in the world, Americans have a special obligation to think this problem through and to begin to find viable alternatives.

• We have a good beginning in new environmental legislation, but this must be followed through vigorously. There are many areas in which we need more and better public regulation and enforcement—conservation of resources, restrictions on pollution emissions, limitations on fertilizers and pesticides, preservation of wilderness areas, protection of animal life. Both government and business have major responsibilities—government to set uniform, effective, and permanent standards, and business to be receptive to such standards and even to take initiative in helping create them.

- Regulation and enforcement are necessary, but frequently as much or more can be accomplished by incentives. At present, our incentives tend to reward those who exploit resources and use the atmosphere and waterways as cost-free disposal systems. Neither heedless exploitation nor pollution can continue, and we must now strive to find ways to reward those who follow ecologically sound pursuits, as well as penalize exploiters and polluters for the damage they cause.

- We must develop new technologies that will allow us to live in harmony with nature while still enjoying the benefits of a modern industrial state. Development of solar heating and power generation, for example, could cut back on one source of pollution and exhaustion of increasingly scarce resources. So, too, the development of efficient and comfortable mass transportation would provide an alternative that would lessen dependence on the automobile, which would save resources and cut back on pollution.

- A stabilized population obviously would help enormously in arresting environmental deterioration. But population distribution is also a factor. Increasingly, we are an urbanized nation. Even if every family makes the decision to have no more than two children, it will take more than sixty years before stabilization—a balance between births and deaths—will be reached. And in that interval there will be a population growth of from 50 to 80 million persons. Even such minimal "built-in" growth will appreciably add to the strain already evident in so many of our urban centers. This creates a need for a whole new range of policies and actions—to upgrade urban centers, to promote expansion of job opportunities in urban areas, to ease the problems of population movement, to increase freedom of choice in residential location, to improve regional and local planning.

• Along with increasing population, increasing affluence is a major contributor to environmental damage under present conditions. The ethic of perpetual economic growth, so pronounced in our society, has been called into question in recent studies, based on the view that on a finite planet growth cannot be infinite. There is substantial and growing agreement on this score among the experts. There is also general agreement that reasonable economic growth will be needed for the future well-being of our society. The real issues have to do with the rate of that growth and its character. Both will require intensive study. To me, one thing is clear now: we must strive to make economic growth more selective and qualitative, with much of the increase devoted to humanistic rather than material considerations.

I believe the prospects are very good for progressively undertaking study and effective action in the foregoing areas. Given the profound significance and underlying nature of the population-environmental challenge, it is heartening to witness the growing awareness of it, the increasing realization that meeting this challenge is an essential precondition to success in so many other problem areas.

What is especially heartening is the realization that the approach is fundamentally based on humanistic values. The Commission on Population Growth and the American Future stated this clearly. It said that "population policy goals must be sought in full consonance with the fundamental values of American life: respect for human freedom, human dignity, and individual fulfillment; and concern for social justice and social welfare."

The orientation is a positive one: to preserve the physical environment that makes human existence possible, to enrich human life, to seek a new and harmonious relationship with nature.

CHAPTER IX

The Self-Renewal of Organizations

THE NEED FOR THE SELF-RENEWAL of organizations is a crucial aspect of the humanistic revolution. Few dimensions of our society affect more people directly and indirectly. American society is highly organized, and many organizations possess extraordinary power. Their man-made environment is of more immediate concern and importance for many citizens than the natural environment.

I am speaking here not only of business corporations and government agencies, but of all kinds of organizations—from Harvard University to General Motors, from the Roman Catholic Church to the U.S. Army, from the AFL–CIO to the Red Cross. American society is characterized by a remarkable diversity and richness of organizations. They are indispensable to modern society, and they have demonstrably accomplished so much on so many fronts. But they all face the issue of self-renewal—of relevancy in a changing environment, of continually reviewing their effectiveness, and, hopefully, their capacity to contribute to the forward motion of our society.

John Gardner eloquently articulated the concept of self-renewal in 1964 in his book *Self-Renewal,* and again in 1970 in *The Recovery of Confidence.* His canvas is the entire society, but he is very clear about the fundamental importance of organizations. His concern is the seemingly inevitable pattern through which many organizations go: birth, growth, and then either permanent rigidity or decay. Gardner's vision is the achieving of "a system or framework within which continuous innovation, renewal, and rebirth can occur." Large organizations often seem stubbornly resistant to positive change and prone to negative forms of change. As Gardner points out: "Renewal is not just innovation and change. It is the process of bringing the results of change in line with our purposes."

I see three purposes in organizational self-renewal: to improve the effectiveness of the organization in accomplishing its own goals; to improve its ability to serve in its own distinctive way the broader public interest; and to improve the environment of the organization for the people who spend so much of their lives within it. Clearly, these purposes are closely interrelated. A broad vision of social responsibility will help an organization change with the times, and therefore improve its ability to pursue its own goals. Heightened commitment and morale among members of the organization obviously will contribute greatly to its effectiveness.

Organizational self-renewal is particularly important during a time of profound social change such as now exists in the United States. As Gardner points out, "A society made up of arteriosclerotic organizations cannot renew itself." The ability of organizations to reflect social change in a responsible manner will have much to do with whether that change is relatively smooth or disruptive. Organizations in our society today, especially large ones, increasingly are becoming a major focus of discontent, with the critics ranging from extremists to responsible analysts and observers.

Externally, the discontent stems from the tendency to place on organizations a large share of the blame for the fact that our social problems appear to be increasing and worsening. Given the fact that organizations have accomplished so much and are so powerful and pervasive in modern life, the argument runs, why haven't they been more effective in solving our problems? The criticisms take many forms, but basically they come down to the view that many organizations either ignore or do not serve well the public interest. They subordinate it to the search for profits or power or self-perpetuation or special interest. To compound this, many believe, organizations tend to erect formidable defenses against anyone or anything which might divert attention from the organization's narrow interests. They become secretive, impersonal, hard to penetrate. The result is that individuals feel powerless vis-à-vis large organizations and come increasingly to see them as part of the problem rather than part of the solution.

Internally, the discontent is based on the view that organizational life is frequently not satisfying or rewarding in human terms. Obviously, organizations have come a very long way from the early stages of the Industrial Revolution, when twelve-hour days, child labor, and inhumane working conditions were the norm. But, as I observed earlier, it is natural that progress only whets the appetite for more progress. Organizational life today is physically more comfortable, but the psychological environment has not improved as much. Organizations, both public and private, are still predominantly bureaucratic, highly structured and regimented, impersonal, characterized by routine and red tape. Employees tend to be seen more as productive units than as people. The goals of the organization are all-demanding. There is great pressure for conformity. The frequent result, many observers believe, is the suppression of human emotion and expression, the stifling of creativity, boredom, timeserving, frustration. This often applies as much to the "organization man" in the white-collar ranks as it does to blue-collar workers on the assembly line.

The current criticism of organizations, of course, is much more varied than I have indicated here. My purpose is not so much to present a full review as it is to suggest how widespread and general it has become. Some critics appear to believe that managers as a class are evil because they do not use their power to change their organizations in ways the critics would like. This betrays a misunderstanding of power—or, more accurately, the *limits* of power—within organizations. There are countless stories of men who have come into top executive positions with an agenda for change, only to find themselves frustrated. An organization is a system, with a logic of its own, and all of the weight of tradition and inertia. The deck is stacked in favor of the tried and proven way of doing things and against the taking of risks and striking out in new directions. In such a system, individual executives, or even groups of executives, often find that their power is far less than their status and level in the organization would suggest.

I certainly do not mean to imply that organizational self-renewal is impossible, only that it is very difficult. It is in this light that I regard the present aura of discontent as healthy, to the extent that it is informed and reasonable. There are many well-motivated managers who would agree completely. Such criticism can become their ally, helping to raise the visibility of issues and aiding them to get others in the organization to see the need for constructive change. In fact, it is not too much to say that a certain amount of turbulence in the atmosphere and the existence of responsible outside criticism are essential to any significant degree of real improvement in the character and performance of large organizations. In a benign and uncomplaining environment, there is little reason to expect managers to be able to bring about any substantial change, given the strength of tradition and organizational defensiveness generally.

Though the classic bureaucratic model is still prevalent, many organizations are beginning to move away from it under the pressure of various forms of change. I see four aspects of change, all bearing on large organizations, all helping to erode the bureaucratic mold, all recent in origin, and all potentially significant in contributing to a continuing process of organizational self-renewal.

One of these aspects is the steady increase in number of professional people working in organizations. This, of course, is related to the numbers of new professions, the increase in size of older professions, and the heightened influence of all of them. The importance lies in the tenacious characteristics of professionalism, some of which run counter to the characteristics of bureaucracy. The abiding loyalty of the professional man is more to his professional group than to the organization in which he happens to be located. This in turn creates a considerable degree of job mobility and hence independence. Further, the professional usually finds his deepest rewards more in personal achievement than in ascending the hierarchical levels of the organization. His status comes more from the esteem in which he is held by his fellow professionals than from rewards the organization can bestow upon him, although the latter are by no means disregarded.

The second changing area is the growing incidence of new, different, and shifting forms of organizational structure within many large corporations and government agencies. This stems from the fact that numerous complex problems cannot be dealt with adequately by conventional bureaucratic structure. So we have project teams, task forces, and temporary groups of many kinds coming together for a specific assignment, then breaking apart when the job is done, with the members going on to other temporary groups within the organization. This approach has become particularly applicable in the new, complex fields, such as aerospace, electronics, defense technology, data processing.

Such practices, of course, differ radically from those of conventional structure. Playing on the word "bureaucracy," Alvin Toffler in *Future Shock* has coined the term "ad-hocracy" for these flexible systems which are so different from the static model of bureaucracy.

The third of the change aspects bearing on organizational life is the experimentation in new organizational forms being carried on largely by young people. Those who make the decision to join large organizations often work for change from within; others attack from outside. But the ways that the young themselves are organizing have not received much attention as yet. Being new and experimental, this phenomenon is not easy to describe. It has its origins in the disinterest of many young people in conventional organizations and very much reflects the "new values." Basically, the main direction seems to be to create a community (rather than a neat organizational form) with a friendly and informal style, collective leadership, respect of members for one another, helping relationships, a rejection of status considerations and control mechanisms, an emphasis on creativity and "doing your own thing."

The last of the four change areas is one I believe to be of extraordinary significance: the human-relations approach to management which numbers of people have been concerned about and worked on over a period of many years. It has matured in recent years, and appears to be based on the startlingly simple proposition that the productivity and stability of an organization are increased over the long run to the extent that its structure, atmosphere, and operating style are in tune with the genuine human interests and needs of its members.

Perhaps the best-known expression of this view appeared in the book *The Human Side of Enterprise* published in 1960 by the late Douglas McGregor, professor of management at MIT and former president of Antioch College. McGregor contrasted "Theory X"—the negative, stern, bureaucratic style of management—with "Theory Y"—a collaborative, positive, and open style of management. Theory X holds that people are basically lazy, selfish, uncreative, that they show little ambition, and constantly will try to take advantage. Therefore managers must supervise closely and coerce people rather than share responsibility. Theory Y, on the other hand, holds that people want to work, take initiative, make decisions, and that creativity is widely, rather than narrowly, distributed among them. The manager's job is to create conditions that will help these qualities emerge.

McGregor points out that a Theory X style functions as a self-fulfilling prophecy—if you treat people as lazy, dull shirkers, that is how they in fact respond. Theory X, McGregor believed, has so predominated in organizational life that we have become habituated to thinking that the behavior it encourages is a true reflection of human nature. The result is that relationships within organizations are often characterized by suspicion, mistrust, one-way communication, empire-building, a "dog-eat-dog" philosophy, a reluctance to share authority, a fear of admitting mistakes.

The writings of human-relations theorists have had a considerable impact on managerial thinking and operating styles. One of them, Warren Bennis, recognized that the responsive chord was already there to be touched, maintaining that the popularity of McGregor's book "was based on his rare empathy for a vast audience of managers who are wistful for an alternative to the mechanistic concept of authority."

This approach to management has been given a boost by linkage with practical methodologies for change, including most importantly the small-group training method (known variously as the T-group, encounter group, sensitivity training, laboratory training, and other names). In employing the group method in organizations, the idea is for employees of various levels to have an opportunity to leave their day-to-day habitat for as long as a week, forming a small group with a new environment to discuss interpersonal relationships and organizational problems. With the help of an experienced social scientist, group members are encouraged to use the new environment to work on such human-relations values as trust, openness, honest communication, creativity, helping relationships, expression rather than suppression of emotion. In this manner, the groups often achieve in a week or less a level of honest communication that otherwise would take months of concerted effort.

The difficulty, of course, is to translate these experiences into everyday operations. This is being done where top management is involved and supportive, and where the group sessions are related to ongoing self-renewal methods. These include the use of consultants, gradual changes in the structure and style of the organization, and shorter versions of the group sessions in which specific job-related tasks are undertaken. A related technique is called "management by objectives," in which those who have the responsibility for carrying out the objectives of any part of the organization participate fully in establishing them.

The four contemporary aspects of change affecting organizations which I have discussed here do not, of course, add up to a coherent surge of organizational self-renewal occurring all across the country. They are separate trends, each with its own characteristics. Nevertheless, they are also congruent, and each is important in stimulating new thinking about how to organize human effort in ways that are both humanistic and effective. It is heartening to perceive them at work and to know that the ingrained routine of many conventional organizations is being changed by a changing environment and wise leadership from within.

The human-relations approach is particularly promising as the management philosophy which can best achieve the purposes of organizational self-renewal, as I outlined them earlier in this chapter. Significantly, this approach is a *management* philosophy, offering perceptive managers not only a sense of direction, but a set of relevant methods for bringing it about.

By definition, the human-relations approach is humanistic—and thus lies within the mainstream of current social change. It sees human beings in all their variety and complexity. It sees that lasting and effective power within organizations is to be found in reason and collaboration rather than in coercion and threat. It therefore reflects the "new values" and creates the prospect that our great organizations may become very much a part of the humanistic revolution.

CHAPTER X

Toward a Humanistic Capitalism

ONE OF THE REASONS why I believe it is accurate to say that a revolution is now under way in the United States is that significant change is occurring not just in isolated instances but in all major dimensions of life. Change today is social, political, and economic, and is affecting all sectors of society—government, business, labor, religion, education.

I have characterized the population-pollution problem as the "underlying" challenge because in the long term it is a matter of survival, and because it functions as an intensifier of so many other problem areas. Other than this, the most crucial area for change in the Second American Revolution, in my judgment, is the economic. If the population-pollution problem is the *underlying* challenge, then change in our economic system is the *overriding* challenge. For at least the next generation, the task of modifying, adjusting, and improving our economic system will be a major preoccupation.

Capitalism has built our country and brought us to an advanced industrial and technological state which is envied throughout the world. But some of the most serious problems our society faces are associated with the humanistic shortcomings of our economic system as it has functioned thus far. I think of poverty, unemployment and underemployment, inflation, pollution, distribution of wealth.

From our agrarian beginnings, we have progressed through a long period of industrialization to become a "postindustrial" society—one which has achieved such an advanced state of economic development that its focus can now shift to humanistic development. Until we reached this point, there was always a rationale for tolerating or explaining away the problems associated with our economic system. They were seen as temporary dislocations, or as conditions that would have to be accepted until we reached a more advanced state of development. Often, it could be said that the benefits of economic progress outweighed the costs of any resulting problems. In the case of those that could not be ignored indefinitely, we undertook such measures as we could to minimize them, but always with the proviso that they not impair economic development.

Now the evidence is strong that we have reached a reckoning point. The problems have matured along with our economy, and they are manifestly serious and pervasive. The challenge before us now is less one of economic development than it is to bring about fundamental changes in our economic system that will in time overcome the problems. Otherwise, their cumulative impact will threaten the economic system itself.

Having majored in economics in college, I at least know enough not to minimize the difficulty and complexity of change in this area. The challenge is a formidable one indeed. But we should recognize one profound and encouraging fact. We have an economic system which is the most productive in the world, in all history. No one, except the most extreme and disaffected elements of our society, is foolish enough to talk about replacing it, since all other known systems have been less successful. If we can preserve the successes and yet change the system to resolve its problems, the revolution in our society will remain nonviolent in nature and our prospects for attaining a desirable future will be immeasurably improved.

Earlier I advanced the view that genuine progress in the years ahead will depend on our ability to achieve a synthesis between the humanistic values of the American Revolution and the values of the industrial state. In respect to our economic system, the hoped-for result of that synthesis might be termed "humanistic capitalism." It would retain many of the basic features of capitalism as we know them today—free enterprise within reasonable restraints for the common good, healthy competition and the creativity it can engender, technological advances, a role for the marketplace, the prospect of material rewards commensurate with one's abilities. But it would operate within a new context, in which the ultimate measure of our economic success will be the extent to which it serves humanistic values. In a time of mounting concern for our fellow men and for our natural environment, our economic system, like other social institutions, will be expected to serve the ends of human development.

A humanistic capitalism will not be brought about by some decisive breakthrough or as the result of a brilliant theory. It will require a great deal of new research and study, careful experimentation, trial and error, education and time. I certainly cannot offer any blueprint. But I do have observations to make on several important areas in which consideration and change are necessary if we are to succeed.

One of these areas is the distribution of wealth. Although in many respects a highly technical subject, this obviously has profound implications and is one of the most difficult issues in any society. The problem is how to preserve incentives and reward differing degrees of talent while, at the same time, assuring a reasonable degree of economic security for all members of the society.

In the Western industrialized nations, the response has been to preserve free enterprise to the maximum extent possible while introducing measures to improve economic distribution. The most important measures include the progressive income tax and inheritance taxes, coupled with philanthropic and government programs designed to assist the economically disadvantaged.

No one should expect such a system to work to everyone's satisfaction. The best one can hope for is that reasonable persons will agree that it is serving the over-all needs of the society adequately. A 1972 study by the Cambridge Institute, a nonprofit research organization, indicates that this approach has not been working as well as many had thought. It appears, for example, that people with higher incomes are paying proportionately less of the total tax burden today than they were twenty years ago. The reason, according to the Cambridge Institute, is that the effective rates of income tax at various income levels have changed hardly at all during that time, while other forms of taxation which impose heavier tax burdens on low incomes (such as the payroll tax and the sales tax) have increased dramatically. The net effect is that lower- and middle-income people are paying more tax in relation to their incomes while upper-income people are paying roughly the same as before. Moreover, the same study indicates that personal ownership of capital, primarily in stocks and bonds, has not varied significantly in the past fifty years. It is still heavily concentrated among a very small percentage of the population.

There are two reasons why this situation has not been a major issue in the years since the end of World War II. One is that it is a very complex subject and there has been insufficient research on it. The other is that our sustained economic growth since the war has served to distract attention from the distribution pattern since it has substantially increased the real income of the great majority in our society, not just the well-to-do. Our society is overwhelmingly middle-class, and the middle class is relatively affluent.

More recently, however, the persistence of such problems as poverty, inflation, and unemployment, and continuing income inequities, as in the case of some minority groups and women, have combined to stir interest anew in the subject of income and capital distribution. It will be a major concern in the years ahead.

Every once in a while, the question will be asked (at least I have been asked it on occasion) : Why not have complete economic equality among all members of society? The answer simply is that it will not work. It would do violence to our ideas of democracy, freedom, free enterprise, and it would destroy incentives. Complete economic equality has never existed anywhere except in small isolated communes. It does not exist in the Soviet Union, nor in Sweden, nor in Israel, which has the most highly developed cooperatives and forms of communal agriculture in the world.

The only viable solution is to do a better job on present methods of income distribution and to find new ways to improve distribution of future economic growth. Certainly, the income tax structure will be a major target for reconsideration. Over the years it has become enormously complicated, with a range of exemptions, credits, and allowances each of which has its reasons and its defenders. For example, I would argue strongly for retention of exemptions for charitable contributions. Such contributions do not benefit the donor monetarily, and they make possible a unique social force in our society, that of philanthropy, which provides a valuable alternative to government in helping to solve our problems.

Tax reform must be approached carefully and responsibly,

from the point of view of the individual who pays taxes, the need for government revenues, and the importance of maintaining, indeed strengthening, private initiative in both the profit and nonprofit sectors. Within this framework, I personally am ready for tax reform which will genuinely ease our problems and move our society forward.

Taxation has its limitations as a method of achieving better economic distribution since for this purpose it is essentially remedial. We must also take a positive approach by finding new ways to spread ownership of future capital growth more broadly in our society. This will be a fertile field for creative ideas and experimentation in the years ahead by both government and the private sector.

One such approach has been developed by Louis Kelso, the California lawyer whose avocation has been economics. In his book *Two-Factor Theory: The Economics of Reality,* Kelso makes a convincing argument that many of the deficiencies of our economic system could be alleviated if ways were found to broaden the ownership of the means of production. The "two factors" are labor and capital. Every working person contributes his labor, but after twenty or thirty or forty years of work relatively few end up owning any share of capital. Kelso proposes a "second income plan" whereby each working person would receive wages for his labor and at the same time accumulate a share of ownership in the enterprise to which he contributes his labor. This has happened in some companies where employee trust funds have financed corporate growth (through bank loans) in return for a block of ownership to be shared by employees. Successful approaches of this sort would pay dividends in terms of employee commitment and morale. And they would not deprive anyone of his present holdings since they are based on future growth.

The second critical area for change in our economic system has to do with the way in which we define the nature of work.

In the industrial age the dominant definition of work is the production of marketable goods and services. From the point of view of the individual, work is predominantly viewed as the price one must pay in order to get in return the material requisites of life. Anyone who does not or cannot conform to these definitions sooner or later comes to be regarded as a social misfit.

In the postindustrial age the question is how we will proceed in broadening the definition of work to include more community service opportunities and pursuits related to individual self-growth. Increasingly, work must come to be viewed as man's opportunity to think, create, and serve, as well as produce.

It is fundamentally important to recognize that work plays a critical role, both psychologically and socially, in the lives of people. To be working provides evidence of being needed—social confirmation. And it helps provide a sense of competence and inner security. The difficulty is that work is not often considered in these ways, but in predominantly economic terms. A key dilemma is whether our system can provide sufficient work opportunities for its citizens which are fulfilling in all three dimensions—the social and psychological as well as the economic.

The nature of the dilemma is not revealed by conventional economic measures, for obvious reasons. It is true that the great majority of what has been defined as the work force has been employed in recent decades. But this says nothing about how rewarding these jobs are or how many of them are make-work jobs or how much featherbedding there is. It is true that in the past work opportunities have always grown at least at the rate of economic growth. But this may not be true in the postindustrial age. The long-term thrust of industrialization and technology is toward replacing human beings by machines in the production of goods and services. Already we see signs of the "rationing" of employment opportunities—prolonged adolescence, four-day weeks, early retirement. To create expanded opportunities, we need very much to develop an expanded definition of work and to alter our system in line with that definition.

Again, there is no single or easy answer, but rather many ways to approach the problem, given time and experimentation and the steady emergence of values that will place a high premium on ways of fostering human growth.

Unfortunately, it is all but impossible to escape the pervasive influence of the marketplace. Anything is called work in our society—doing esoteric research, playing the flute, making patchwork quilts, playing basketball—as long as somebody will pay the practitioner enough to fulfill his needs for food, clothing, and shelter. This suggests that a large part of the answer lies within existing economic institutions, which are already coping rather well with the demands of the marketplace. To the extent that business firms take a broader view of their responsibility in helping to meet social problems (as I discuss in the next chapter) they will also be broadening their view of work. They will be creating new interests and new jobs—many of which will meet the desires of employees to make a contribution to society.

The other avenue within existing economic institutions is the one I discussed in the last chapter—bringing conventional work more in line with human needs and aspirations. Just one among many possibilities is encouraging a return to a spirit of craftsmanship—a sense of accomplishment and pride in one's work. I noted with interest the recent experiments of the Volvo and Saab companies in Sweden. In place of routine and repetitive work, a team of workmen builds an entire unit, taking pride in the product of their skill. And I noted with equal interest that the attempt to speed up an assembly line in an automobile plant in Ohio resulted in a near-revolt by assembly line workers. These two cases raise the question of productivity, the importance of which I fully recognize in terms of meeting our social needs. I believe that one of the most promising routes to increasing productivity will be to improve the commitment and morale of employees by making jobs more satisfying to the individual worker.

It is likely that we will see significant progress in such approaches in the business world because it is in the long-run best interests of both the companies and their employees. It will mean that the companies will be moving with, rather than against, the growing desires of people to find work that is fulfilling in human terms. It will also call on organized labor for greater flexibility in its economic demands where less tangible but equally vital humanistic gains can result. This cannot fail to be profitable in the fullest sense of the word, for business and labor alike.

It is outside existing economic institutions that the broadening of work opportunities will be perhaps the most difficult and challenging. The situation is somewhat ironic. On the one hand, we have growing unmet needs in health care, the environment, safety, transportation, social service, education, beautification, and many other areas. On the other hand, we have growing numbers of people who would find service opportunities in these areas challenging and rewarding. But we have not been able to do an adequate job of putting the needs and the labor together in viable programs that will pay a living wage.

It seems to me that we have to begin to think about large-scale programs to meet this need through creative and cooperative action—by government, business, labor and the private nonprofit sector. We need leadership in identifying genuine service opportunities and in designing imaginative programs that will make it possible for people interested in those opportunities to work on them.

The WPA experience during the Great Depression of the

1930s is instructive when we think of large-scale job-creating programs. Despite significant accomplishments, the WPA often suffered from a "make-work" aura because it was a job program of last resort. But if the needs are real and people with high motivation are available, there is no reason whatsoever for the aura to be negative. The Peace Corps and VISTA did not suffer from this. The point is that we should be generative rather than reactive—we should build in a positive aura by being farsighted and creating opportunities before the problems become manifestly acute.

If we start in this direction, I believe there will be no dearth of ideas. A recent one, for example, is to create a new job program for people to assist in work on preserving and restoring historical sites throughout the Bicentennial era. In terms of grants or other forms of support for individual endeavors, the needs are almost endless in such areas as research, the arts, and public service. A fertile field will be the encouragement of cooperatives of many kinds—agricultural, marketing, consumer, housing. In aggregating the economic power of low- and middle-income people, cooperatives usually create capital which is used to develop new services and therefore new jobs. Such jobs are often very attractive in terms of social-service opportunities. A related field is community development corporations. They are similar to cooperatives except that the organizing principle is primarily geographic in that the residents of a town or neighborhood or city come together to create an organization which may take on a broad range of community development projects.

The third area of change I want to discuss deals with the ethic of perpetual economic growth, and the standards by which economic activity is measured. I touched on this subject earlier, indicating my belief that there can be no question of stopping economic growth, but that we should concern ourselves very much with the character of that growth.

It is clear that the two areas of change I have already discussed in this chapter—better distribution of wealth and a broadened definition of work—will depend very much on continued economic growth. But as I stressed in a speech to The Conference Board in February 1971, we must strive to achieve selective, qualitative, and orderly economic growth—emphasizing quality over quantity, a concern for the environment, better economic distribution, managerial skill of the highest order.

We need to shift the priorities of growth toward, for example, more and better homes and schools, instead of toward faster airplanes and more destructive weapons. And, as it gradually becomes possible to lessen the rate of increase of growth of a material kind, growth should accelerate in the great humanistic and social endeavors—health, education, art, music, literature, philosophy, basic scientific research.

Encouraging economic growth of the kind I have described will require new standards of measurement. Virtually all of the indices of business activity currently used are based on volume, with the Gross National Product being only the most prominent. These indices are conducive to the mental set that more is better. We need new economic and social indicators that measure quality. There have been efforts both in the government and in the private sector to begin to work toward developing such indices, and what has been learned so far is chiefly that it is a very difficult task. But it must be pursued with renewed commitment if we are going to be able to assess how economic activity does or does not contribute to the quality of life.

The final area on which I wish to make some comments is the critical and nagging issue of poverty. It is much more than an embarrassment in an affluent country—it is a human tragedy for those afflicted and a social and economic loss to the total society.

One prime goal of the humanistic revolution is to create a society in which there is full opportunity for every member to contribute to the society and to feel wanted and needed in return. Clearly those who are poverty-stricken—many stigmatized by the present welfare system—do not feel any such reciprocal relationship. They feel locked into the poverty cycle in which parents are too poor to provide their children with the proper food, enriching home life, and incentives to learn, which would enable them to break out.

I believe that progress in the three change areas I have already discussed will serve to greatly reduce the poverty problem. But these effects will take considerable time, and in the interim poverty will decline at a very slow rate unless we take some decisive action to ameliorate it. The best prospect seems to lie in some form of the guaranteed annual income. This at least would assure that minimal needs were met, and, like Social Security, would greatly lessen the stigma and expensive administrative costs of the present welfare systems.

I realize, of course, that there are many who have doubts about a guaranteed annual income, fearing that it would create an enormous class of drones. More and more people, however, are beginning to take a positive view of human nature, to understand that most people want to be productive and needed, want a sense of community and of self-esteem, want, in short, to work. There will always be exceptions, but I am confident that there will be far fewer drones than many of us think, and that removing the fear of financial insecurity may well release new sources of creativity and energy.

A 1972 Brookings Institution study by social scientist Leonard Goodwin answers the question posed by its title—*Do the Poor Want to Work?*—with a strong affirmative. Intensive research, including survey data, disclosed that welfare recipients have essentially the same work ethic and life aspirations as do middle-class people. In fact, the stronger the work ethic of welfare recipients, the more likely they are to be overwhelmed by evidence of failure. What they need is active encouragement, basic economic security, and opportunities to achieve status and experience success.

In commenting on these four areas in which change will be necessary if we are to move toward a humanistic capitalism, I am certainly not posing as an economist. But in the new spirit of "economics being too important to be left to the economists," I have felt compelled to deal with this difficult subject. Economists by themselves cannot make the decisions about the future shape and character of our economic system. That is our job, the job of us the citizens, the total society. It is up to us to determine the kind of future we want, what we expect from our economic system in the years ahead, and the values that are really important to us. If we can do this, we will be providing a sense of direction, a context, within which economists and others can go to work to carry out the research and experimentation and development that will be necessary if we are to achieve a humanistic capitalism.

CHAPTER XI

Corporate Responsibility

THROUGHOUT THIS BOOK I have supported the thesis that we in the United States are in the early stages of a revolution. Clearly, a revolution is not a time for business-as-usual.

There is perhaps no single group in the country which finds itself more directly at the crossroads of critical choice than business leadership. On the one hand, business leaders have a great deal to lose if social change sours and degenerates into social breakdown. On the other, they have a great deal to contribute—and to gain—in helping in positive ways to build a better society.

In recent years the business community has increasingly been called upon to help deal with social problems, a challenge that has come to be known as "corporate responsibility." The emergence of this concept is in itself one barometer of how difficult our problems have become and how sweeping are the currents of change. Only a decade ago it would have seemed odd to think of business as being responsible for anything more than producing the goods and services that people need, creating jobs,

91

paying fair wages, ensuring worker safety, earning a decent profit, and doing all of this in a lawful and reasonable manner.

Since the Civil War it has not been often that business was very popular. One has only to think of the age of trust-busting, of the time of the emergence of trade unions, and of the Depression. But during World War II and until very recently business has enjoyed a high reputation and an unusual position of power and respect in the society.

The United States came out of World War II as the most powerful nation on earth, and virtually everyone attributed that in large measure to the skill and ingenuity of American business and its productivity. Since then, except for several relatively brief recessions, we have had a twenty-five-year economic boom. There were great technological advances, and business made them widely available. American managerial techniques have been admired and emulated the world over. The business schools flourished and young people in great numbers set out for careers in technology and business. Who, it seemed, could ask for anything more?

Now a great deal more is being asked as a new perspective begins to emerge. The due-bill on pollution is being tallied. The consumerism movement indicates the growing skepticism that government and business are doing an adequate job of ensuring that all products are safe and fairly advertised. The persistence of such problems as unemployment, poverty, and inflation creates doubts about our economic system. Many of the brightest young people now seem to be turning away from business careers. The near-collapse of Lockheed and the Penn Central bankruptcy debacle undermine the widespread view that private business represents the ultimate in skill and efficiency. Critics have become fond of reminding businessmen that their position in society is a privileged one and not immutable, that business has a responsibility for helping to solve society's problems.

How are businessmen responding to these new pressures and manifest problems? Several years ago an astute business leader on the West Coast was forthright in a comment he made to me. He said that far too many businessmen "don't even know it's raining." Since then I have had occasion to discuss the growing criticism of business with a number of corporate executives from different parts of the country. My perception is that more and more business leaders realize that times are changing and that they must begin to carefully reconsider their proper role and responsibilities in the new situation. Yet despite the growing dialogue on "corporate responsibility," my observation is that as yet few business leaders have reached clear conclusions, and even fewer have taken decisive action.

Increasingly, the widespread view in our society today is that those characteristics of business which I mentioned earlier—providing goods and services, creating jobs, paying fair wages, and so on—are only the starting point. The difficult question inherent in the challenge of corporate responsibility is: How far beyond these characteristics should business go in helping to resolve the problems of our society?

Broadly speaking, there are two answers to the question. The first and more limited one is that corporations should be expected to do only that for which they are clearly and directly responsible and for which they feel competent. The ideal level of performance within this first view would include the following:

- Taking all reasonable steps in internal management to make working conditions congruent with human needs—trying to encourage development of the human potential of employees rather than seeing them only as one of the means of production.
- Making sure that products are safe, nonpolluting, and fairly advertised.

- A readiness to live up to the spirit, as well as the letter, of government regulations and laws in such areas as fair employment and environmental protection.
- Playing fully the role of good citizen in communities where home offices and major installations are located—a concern for the total welfare of the community, encouraging employees to participate in community affairs, responding to local charities, and the like.
- A positive "new business" attitude toward invitations from the government and other sources to participate in the solution of social problems when the company's background and expertise seem relevant.

These areas of responsibility obviously cover a great deal of ground. If every company in the United States fulfilled them, our situation would be vastly improved. A good case can be made that this is enough to expect of business.

And yet it is a limited view, for it rests basically on the assumption that business is not competent to deal with many of the problems facing our society, that it should stick to areas in which it has tested and proved managerial and technical competence. But I would ask: Who *is* competent to deal with these problems? Surely no one sector alone—not government, not business, not labor, not education, not the nonprofit sector. The nature of the challenges which confront us today transcends the competence of any one sector, but not of all if each played an active and committed part.

The limited approach to corporate responsibility by the business community will not sufficiently influence the currents of social change in positive directions. Nor will it sufficiently unleash the powers of creativity and imagination to achieve a real breakthrough in resolving our social problems.

The second view of corporate responsibility calls for the business community not only to perform well within its own purview and areas of competence, but to go beyond them, to take initiative and to collaborate with government and other sectors of society in full and active and dedicated participation to help come to grips with the great problems that confront us. We desperately need the ingenuity, the flexibility, the expertise of the business community in a posture of active leadership and involvement. We need businessmen who are willing to go beyond the ordinary and the obvious, men who have the courage and vision to seek new ways of involvement, men who are committed to the total well-being of our society.

I am well aware of the dangers of "great expectations." Arjay Miller, dean of the Stanford Business School and former president of the Ford Motor Company, has made the point cogently that it would be a tragic mistake to transfer to the business community the same high hopes and expectations for solving our problems as the Federal Government has been burdened with in recent decades.

To expect any one sector to bear the brunt of problem-solving amounts to nothing less than an evasion of responsibility by the other sectors and by all of us as individual citizens. But it would also be a tragic mistake to expect too little.

Clearly, in making a commitment to be socially responsible in the fullest sense, no corporation can go so far that it neglects its own basic health and stability. Every corporation must concern itself with profits, with success in the conventional business sense, not only for the sheer sake of survival but because a strong and vigorous business community is fundamental to the well-being of the society. Moreover, no company can be effective in meeting its social responsibilities if it cannot meet its business responsibilities. The challenge is to be successful in business *and* in serving the needs of the society. Is it unreasonable to assume that the same abilities and qualities apply in both cases? I think not.

A major characteristic of the expanded view of corporate

responsibility would be efforts to bring about changes in our economic system that would in themselves benefit the society or would enhance the corporation's ability to serve.

For example, corporate initiative is very much needed in two areas that I discussed in the last chapter. One is the development of new standards of measurement that would go beyond the strictly economic. The other is the need for finding ways to spread the benefits of capitalism more widely, to make it possible for employees to earn a share of ownership for their labor in addition to wages.

Another example has to do with changes in the antitrust laws to allow for concerted actions by corporations toward socially responsible goals. These might include antipollution programs and a cooperative method of deciding on new plant locations, having in mind population-distribution problems and regional economic patterns. Today, too many businessmen take refuge behind the antitrust laws as an excuse for avoiding concerted action. These laws are probably much less of a barrier than they are often made out to be. Where they genuinely need changing for social purposes, businessmen should take the lead in proposing such change. Additionally, where a social goal can be pursued successfully only through governmental action, the exercise of corporate responsibility should take the form of business support for the necessary legislation.

Another element of corporate responsibility at its best would be measures to help close the credibility gap in corporate performance. By this I mean that the chief source of information about corporate responsibility is the advertising and public-relations activities of the corporations themselves. Improved standards of measurement would certainly improve the situation. Other ideas for providing objective information and thereby improving corporate performance and credibility should be given serious consideration, such ideas as appointing public members to boards of directors and commissioning outside and impartial studies of corporate programs.

One very specific way that corporations can increase their ability to serve the needs of society is in the area of philanthropic contributions. Under existing tax laws, corporations are able to deduct up to 5 percent of net income before taxes for charitable contributions. Most corporations take some advantage of this provision, chiefly in their community-relations programs and in supporting higher education. A few corporations have varied, balanced, and extensive programs of charitable contributions, using the full 5 percent provision.

However, the average contribution for all corporations has consistently hovered around *one* percent in recent years. For the most part, the contributions are made to causes and programs which can reasonably be related back to the corporation's own interests. It is not an exaggeration to say that much of corporate philanthropy can be classified as an adjunct of corporate public relations. A great deal of corporate giving is tokenism, or is seen basically in defensive terms.

If substantial numbers of corporations recognize the potential importance of their philanthropic programs, if they concentrate them more on significant social needs and increase the amount of their giving to achieve greater impact, what a vast difference it will make.

As I shall discuss in a later chapter, the nonprofit sector of American society—comprising thousands of institutions in such fields as social service, education, culture, the arts—is in serious financial difficulty. In addition, many new nonprofit organizations are coming into existence to deal with new and pressing problems. This has placed a serious overload on the traditional sources of philanthropic funds.

The result, it seems to me, is an unprecedented opportunity for business to demonstrate a concern for the total society, to see the needs that are unmet, to recognize the necessity of maintaining a healthy and balanced pluralism.

In Cleveland, Ohio, some years back, a number of companies joined a plan calling for each to give one percent of their net income before taxes to higher education each year. As a model for increasing corporate giving, this could be followed by other companies in other cities. Might not this one percent for education be supplemented in due course with another one percent for social-service programs? And then later another one percent could be added for the arts, thus gradually leading toward the full 5 percent on a planned basis. This would be implementing the true spirit of corporate responsibility, with consequences that would be unbelievably significant.

I believe that the time has come when businessmen should view corporate responsibility not in a limited or narrow way, but in an expansive and open way—as their opportunity to both serve their own long-term interests and contribute to the betterment of society. The basic point I would underscore is the fundamental need for understanding and commitment and leadership within the business community itself. Change that comes from within is far more likely to be genuine and lasting and creative than change that occurs only in response to outside pressure.

I do not mean to underplay the role of constructive outside criticism and pressure from whatever source—consumers, the press, government. The outside stimulus is needed to raise the visibility of issues, to provide a new perspective. The daily lives of businessmen are very full in the competitive struggle for success. In this situation, they are much more likely to give priority to social problems if their environment influences them to do so with loud and clear signals.

A defensive or limited response will only intensify the outside pressure. How much better it would be for business leaders to take the initiative now rather than find themselves forced to act in the future by some authoritarian figure or under pressure from extremist factions. The hope is that businessmen increasingly will come to understand that their own future is inextricably bound up with that of the total society, that doing an adequate job within a limited frame of reference is no longer enough. Now is the time to go beyond business-as-usual, to see and to respond to the needs of the community and the nation.

Corporate responsibility in the fullest sense will not occur overnight. It will require a patient, long-term effort, beginning in many cases with small beginnings, and going from there to larger tasks. The watchers and critics of business must understand that miracles and grand solutions are not very likely, that in many cases corporate responsibility will be best manifested initially in actions that are local and specific. As I have said before, they must understand, too, the limits of power. Bureaucracy can be as formidable a factor in business as it is in government. Very often top executives will see the need for greater involvement in social problems, but are thwarted by cautious boards of directors or by middle managers who feel threatened by new rules of the game.

I have confidence in a long-term process of constructive outside criticism and growing response and initiative within the ranks of business. I believe that more and more businessmen are coming to see their own self-interest and that of their companies in larger terms than sales quotas and the balance sheet. They are recognizing as never before the interrelationship between the success of their companies and the well-being of the society in which they operate, that unless they help the society to solve its problems, their companies cannot succeed in the long run.

CHAPTER XII

The Role of Government

IN SEEKING WAYS to move our society forward in humanistic directions, a vitally important consideration is the role of the Federal Government.

The most obvious reason for this is a truism I need not belabor: the steadily growing power and dominance of government throughout the society. That power consists of much more than sheer numbers of dollars and personnel, as important as they are. It also lies in the classic functions of government, which are enormously heightened in significance during a time of stress and strong pressures for change. Particularly relevant among those functions today is government's ultimate authority to hold back or sanction the forces of change.

Such power quite naturally breeds strong feelings. There is a great deal of criticism of the government, some mistrust, and even fear. Many see an inexorable trend toward statism and bureaucracy, toward a remoteness from the people—in place of the pluralism and diversity that have always been such a strong characteristic of American life.

But even those who are most concerned about the growing power of government often find themselves urging the government to do more, for lack of a better alternative. This is especially true of young people, who are among the most severe critics of government institutions and processes. The same young people, when pressed on what they would do to solve our problems, often end up by talking about what government should do.

Partly because of the complexity of our situation, it is extremely difficult to find alternatives to the steady growth of government. Political scientists and other social critics have begun to focus increasingly on the issue of the role of government in the years ahead, but I think it is fair to say that no clear answer has yet permeated the public consciousness. It seems to me of urgent necessity to try to clarify whether or not we have any viable alternative to the steady accretion of centralized power.

A useful prelude is to review the way the role of government has evolved over our two-hundred-year history. For Americans have always debated this issue and have always tried to influence the nature and power of their government, so deeply ingrained in our system is the doctrine that government should be the servant, not the master, of the people. In the light of this, it is gratifying to realize that in the past the government has generally reflected the dominant concerns and issues of each era.

Beginning with the adoption of the Constitution, the first important role of the government was *formative* in nature. During this period the preoccupation was with getting the newly designed Federal machinery established and operating. In 1789 occurred the election of the first President and the first sitting of the Congress and the Supreme Court. Soon the Bill of Rights was added to the Constitution, thereby allaying the concern of many people over centralization of power in the new national government. Political parties, though not provided for in the Constitution, emerged to provide the external process needed to enable the new Federal machinery to operate. And early debate over the effective functioning of the Constitution triggered a clarification of the powers of the Supreme Court. Its declaration of the doctrine of judicial review established the judicial branch as a full equal of the other two. This was also a formative period in foreign affairs. Diplomatic relations, as well as patterns of trade and commerce, were established with foreign governments.

It is important to note that throughout this period such key leaders as Washington, Jefferson, Madison, Hamilton, and Marshall all had a profound sense of the importance of their actions in setting significant precedents for future generations.

The next major role the government played in the development of the nation was *territorial expansion.* In the period from the Louisiana Purchase in 1803 through the purchase of Alaska in 1868, the United States expanded to its present territorial boundaries and in the process more than tripled in size. In addition to acquiring these lands, the government played an important part in settling and developing them. Through such measures as granting parcels of land to homesteaders, miners, and the railroads, the government fostered a continuous westward migration of its Eastern citizenry.

The third major role the government played was that of *preserving the Union.* Starting with the election of Andrew Jackson in 1828, the nation again turned its attention to the problems of man in society. In words that are relevant today, one writer described the age of Jackson as "a time when every man carried in his pocket a plan for Utopia, calling for reform of the relations of man to man or of society to man." Jackson was the first President to come from outside the thirteen original states, and his Administration reflected the robust egalitarianism of the common man and the frontier. Organized labor had its beginnings during this period, rallying around three issues—a "ten-hour day," easing the treatment of debtors, and free education for all.

As tensions between reformers and the "establishment" grew, the greatest social problem in American history—slavery—became the overriding issue. The problem of maintaining a national consensus came to a head with the election of Lincoln. South Carolina seceded, and other Southern states followed, primarily to support the principle of the right of a state to secede if it found itself unable to live with policies established by the national government. The old Federalist contention that a national government was necessary to protect the rights of citizens to life, liberty, and the pursuit of happiness was again put to the test, only this time a war rather than a vote was required for its ratification.

Following the cessation of the conflict and the painful restoration of the Union, government played another major role in the development of the nation, that of fostering *industrialization*. In the thirty-five-year period from the end of the Civil War to the beginning of the twentieth century, America changed from an agricultural economy to an industrial power. The hand of government was everywhere. It continued, through land grants and other means, to support the expansion of the transportation network necessary for industrial growth. It legitimized the innovation needed for the growth of industrial capitalism—the limited-liability corporation. It protected our fledgling industries from the competition of older, foreign producers through tariffs. It provided the necessary labor by encouraging immigration, and it afforded incentives for the invention of the necessary tools through the patent system.

At the end of the nineteenth century government emerged in a new role, that of the *economic stabilizer*. Beginning with the passage of the Sherman Anti-Trust Act in 1890, through the

New Deal, and down to the Keynesian theories of recent times, the government has functioned as a sort of balance wheel in the evolution of the American economy.

As indicated above, the government supported the growth of the large corporations. But as time passed and protests against the size and power of the corporations grew, the government set up machinery to regulate business practices. It also came to the support of labor with the passage of the Wagner Act in 1935, which set the stage for labor to take its place at the bargaining table as an equal partner with management. And when a series of crises threatened to displace millions of farmers and seriously curtail agricultural production, the government responded with a series of programs, including subsidies, educational support, and technical assistance. When the whole economic system began to collapse during the Depression, the government entered the economy directly—as an employer (WPA and CCC), as a producer of needed but as yet privately unprofitable goods and services (TVA and REA), and as a regulator of business cycles through price, wage, and monetary controls. What started out as a big-business system ended up as an intricate set of checks and balances among big business, big labor, and big government.

Another major governmental role, one that has preoccupied us during most of this century, is concerned with *international status and security*. First there was our imperialistic period, leading up to the Spanish-American War, and continuing for a number of years afterward. The United States had emerged as a world power, and was to be irresistibly and often reluctantly drawn into the arena of international conflict. Originally pledged to avoid foreign entanglements, the United States ultimately found that the "fortress America" concept was not a sufficient answer to the problems of a shrinking and increasingly interdependent world.

As early as 1823 an American President, James Monroe,

thought it necessary to warn aggressively-inclined European monarchs that not only the United States but the whole American continent was no longer a field for colonialism. Nearly one hundred years later another American President, Woodrow Wilson, at first tried to avoid involvement in World War I, but he and the entire nation soon found that the world had become too small and interdependent, that they had no real choice.

The United States came out of the war the least damaged of any of the participants and immediately assumed the role of peacemaker. Despite Wilson's heroic efforts, a resurgence of American isolationism defeated his attempt to persuade Congress to approve U.S. membership in the League of Nations. Only a little more than a generation later we found ourselves in World War II.

Again the United States emerged victorious and relatively unimpaired. But again peace has proved elusive. World tensions have continued almost unabated throughout the postwar period. We are still devoting more than a third of our national budget to security and related foreign affairs expenditures.

Coming to the present time, the Federal Government began actively to assume another major role in addition to those of security and economic stabilizer. It began to attempt to *manage social change,* as many domestic problems became manifestly serious. This was foreshadowed, of course, in the Roosevelt era, and in the 1950s with the school desegregation and other decisions of the Warren Court. But it reached its apex in the 1960s in President Lyndon B. Johnson's "Great Society" programs. Civil rights legislation was passed, and initiatives were undertaken to deal with the effects of such problems as urbanization and population growth. Expenditures increased for health and education and Social Security, and new programs were launched to cope with poverty and pollution and crime.

This historical review demonstrates, I believe, that in the past the processes of democracy have worked. The Federal Government has responded to the needs and desires of the society. The point is not that the government has never acted unwisely, moved late, persisted too long, or been ineffective. It has done all of these at one time or another—but it has responded.

Any satisfaction we take from this realization, however, should be tempered. It is dangerous to make the comfortable assumption that because something has happened in the past it will necessarily happen again. This is in itself one reason why it is urgent for us now to take initiative in reconsidering the role of government.

There are other reasons. I have already referred to the steady accumulation of power by the government, resulting in a basic imbalance among the three broad sectors of our society, government, business, and the private nonprofit sector. The first is very powerful, the second is strong, and the third is weak. But beyond this imbalance, it is also clear that the most recent role of government—as manager of social change—has not worked. The problems are not getting solved. A major study by the Brookings Institution in 1972, which was termed by the press a "formal epitaph for the Great Society," came down hard on this point. It described the approach prevalent in the 1960s—the belief that if a problem could be identified and enough Federal money allocated, the problem eventually would be solved. The study demonstrated convincingly that all too often direct action by the government and the spending of large sums of Federal money only made the problems worse.

At first glance, the notion that greater effort by the government to deal with our social problems might in some cases be ineffective and in others even counterproductive seems to fly in the face of logic. Yet the same point has been made increasingly in recent years by other analysts and observers, based more on intuition than on research and data as in the case of the Brookings study.

One major factor that has often been pointed out is government bureaucracy. In some cases, I am told, bureaucratic "layering" has been so massive that only 40 percent of appropriated funds actually reaches those involved directly in the social problem which the money is appropriated to resolve. We have been piling program on top of program. At one time, there were more than four hundred separate grant-in-aid programs relating to urban problems.

Another factor is the sheer overload on government. We all know how strong the tendency has been in recent years to see government as "the employer of last resort," as the only recourse for handling "uneconomic" problems, as the only force in the nation powerful enough to deal with our grave social ills. As a result, the Federal Government has taken on responsibility for almost every problem that could be named.

Still another reason why the steady growth of government has not proved effective in meeting our problems is the psychological effect the growth has had on other sectors of society. Placing increasing responsibility on government for problem-solving has the inevitable effect of lessening the sense of responsibility in these other sectors. As I have already said, it is becoming more and more clear that every sector must take its share of responsibility and play its full role if we are to succeed.

The conclusion of the Brookings study was not that we should stand aside and let the problems fester or that the government should stop spending money on social problems. Rather, it held that government action was not based sufficiently on knowledge and tough-minded experimentation to be able to find viable alternatives. The study also stressed that there was not enough emphasis on developing incentives to encourage private-sector involvement.

The Brookings study and other analyses seem to me to provide some obvious clues to the new directions the Federal

Government must take in the 1970s and beyond. The findings reinforce my own belief that we need to conserve and regenerate what is unique to our system—the power of individual initiative. The time has come to go to our basic strength—the involvement and commitment of the people in all their multifarious capacities and talents.

We need a deliberate, consistent, long-term policy to decentralize and privatize many government functions—to share power, to diffuse power throughout the society. Such a policy must be guided by wise leaders, fostered by an able public service, and draw on all elements of the society. In short, the government must strive to "turn on" the private sector. Its new role must be that of *facilitator of participation*.

This approach is essentially conservative. But I do not mean the brand of conservatism that went under the heading of "states' rights" in the 1950s and 1960s, which, as Adlai Stevenson pointed out so aptly, was really a cover for "states' wrongs," such as segregation. Rather, the approach is conservative in the sense of rekindling the historic elements of strength in our system. If Americans want another type of governmental and social system, I would hope that we could make that choice consciously and deliberately, rather than simply drifting into a new system. But it seems to me that drifting toward a new system is exactly what is happening under our present course. The steady growth of centralized government must ultimately result in a statist and bureaucratic pattern quite unlike anything we have known in the past. The only alternative is for government and other sectors of society to collaborate in leading us back to a balanced system, based on the bedrock of individual initiative.

I am, of course, not implying that such an alternative amounts to the government's simply relinquishing power or returning to a golden age. The world is much too complex for that and our problems much too serious. We need to be inventive about a whole range of ways in which the Federal Government can delegate powers to other levels of government, design new public-private approaches, and develop incentives for private action. It should be clear that the power still ultimately resides with the government in the sense that incentives can always be reversed and delegated powers recalled.

Decentralization refers specifically to levels of government—sharing Federal power with the state and local levels. This is one major direction in which we should go. There are many ways to decentralize. The most recent idea in this area is revenue-sharing, the proposal for one level of government to share its tax revenue with another. A well-conceived and consistent drive to decentralize will not be an easy route, but a very promising one. It is not just a matter of turning over money. I stressed this in a talk at the Rockefeller Public Service Awards luncheon of 1968:

> Decentralization is no panacea in itself, but rather a very complex process in which the Federal Government will still bear responsibility for seeing that its resources and powers produce results.

I also pointed out that to make any appreciable measure of decentralization workable, much would have to be done to strengthen the competence of state and local governments to discharge heavier responsibilities, including "building strong and able public services."

"Privatizing" refers to moving as many government functions and responsibilities toward the private sector as possible, with suitable ground rules and conditions. New organizational forms must be developed to combine the best features of the public and private sectors—accountability, responsibility for the public interest, and the legitimization factor on the government side, with the flexibility, energy, and innovation which characterize the private sector at its best. And there should be renewed emphasis on such traditional means of involving the private sector, both profit and nonprofit, as contracts, grants, tax incentives. Also important are government-managed efforts which rely mainly on private talent in the manner of NASA, but directed toward social problems. Another tool would be simply the removal of inhibitions to private action by changing regulatory or legislative provisions. An example would be modifying the antitrust laws to make possible industry-wide action on social problems, as discussed in the last chapter.

Of course, there has already been a good deal of experimentation with new quasi-public organizational forms (quasi-private would be just as good a term). Most have public-private boards, but they have differing methods of accountability, differing degrees of dependency on government and private funding, different types of charters.

COMSAT is a well-known example, combining government-funded space technology with private funds (one-half of the stock was sold to the public) for civilian applications of communications satellites. Thus far it has been a successful venture.

Another example of older vintage is the Federal National Mortgage Association, which was "privatized" in 1968 when all its stock was sold to the public. Since then its staff has been reduced, even though the volume of work has risen steadily.

Another variation to achieve some measure of the flexibility characteristic of the private sector is the case of the Postal Service, transformed in 1971 from a government agency to the status of a public utility. It is still too new to evaluate, but already it seems clear that the debilitating factor of political patronage in key jobs is being steadily eliminated, thereby greatly improving employee morale. The eventual goal, of course, is to make the Service more efficient and, at the same time, self-supporting financially.

The existence of these and other new public-private organizations should not be construed to mean that the new role of government I am advocating is assured, only that it may be emerging in its early stages. This is obvious when the experimentation in public-private forms to date is compared with the full range of government powers and activities today.

I should also make clear that I am not proposing the dismantling of government agencies and a reversal of government's financial involvement in social problems. Rather, I am saying that action on behalf of the public interest should be a two-way street, not only a matter of new responsibilities gravitating to government, but also the reverse—government striving to find ways to increase the involvement of the private sector. There has been a strong tendency in the first direction. Now we need to emphasize the other direction, not just for the sake of balance, but also for effectiveness. We need new approaches and a new orientation, that of *facilitator of participation*—finding new methods of partnership with other levels of government and other sectors of society, to bring all our strength to bear on problem-solving.

Also important to stress, as the Brookings study implies, is greater experimentation and development of new knowledge. The costs may well be substantial. It will be up to the government to support research and development for social problems much as it has done in the past for the defense and space industries.

All the foregoing actions and innovations that would contribute to the new role of the Federal Government obviously can only spring from a shift in attitude, from a new spirit of collaboration and participation both within the government and among the public generally. I tried to suggest some of the elements of that new spirit in commenting on the future of the public service in the 1968 talk I referred to earlier in this chapter. At that time I said: "The public service is now in an era when

- Effectiveness is more important than efficiency.
- Doing a job is less important than creating conditions that encourage others to do the job.
- People and their problems are more important than agencies and their functions.
- Caution is less important than open, direct confrontation.
- Human-relations skills require more attention than technical skills."

I think these comments make clear my belief that the new era would be one in which the public service becomes not less significant but rather substantially more rewarding and more challenging.

To me, the role of government as *facilitator of participation* would be consistent with all the dimensions of the Second American Revolution. It would be a role necessarily characterized by trust and collaboration and openness—with the humanistic base of the "new values." It would help regenerate the fundamental strength of the American system, the strength of individual initiative. It would help turn back the sense of alienation and powerlessness that grips so many today.

And, for all these reasons, it would simply be the most effective role that the government could play in our time.

CHAPTER XIII

A Giving Society

ONE FUNDAMENTAL WAY I would describe the society I see emerging from the Second American Revolution is that it would be a giving society. A spirit of giving, to something bigger than one's self and without expectation of material reward, would be a major characteristic throughout that society. It seems to me that such a spirit is at the heart of the "new values" I discussed earlier.

In its broadest meaning, philanthropy comes very close to the concept of a giving society. Its Greek root means literally "love of mankind." But for working purposes in this chapter I will speak of philanthropy in the generally understood and more limited sense of the giving of financial assistance for specific worthwhile ends. In this sense, philanthropy is a major component of a giving society.

The giving society also embraces the thousands of nonprofit organizations of immense diversity and variety of purpose—from the Kiwanis to "Nader's Raiders," from the Boy Scouts to the American Civil Liberties Union, from colleges and churches to hospitals and libraries and symphony orchestras. And, most fundamentally of all, it embraces the initiative of individual people, their willingness to give of themselves—their ideas, energies, resources—to worthwhile and constructive activities for the common good.

In a sense, I was born into philanthropy in that material resources far beyond my own needs were to be entrusted to me, and certain values were inculcated at an early age. One was that these resources were to be seen less as a personal possession than as a trust to be used as effectively as possible in efforts to promote human welfare. The word "stewardship" was often used by my father, I remember. Another value was that to be effective one must not merely give away money, but become personally involved—giving not only resources, but of one's self. To me, the core of giving is initiative, involvement, and commitment. If this is true, then the magnitude of the resources at one's disposal becomes less important than the willingness to become involved.

Discussing the elements of a giving society—philanthropy, nonprofit organizations, individual initiative—is made difficult by the lack of precise definitions and terms. For the most part I will simply use the term "private nonprofit," for want of something better and with confidence that the reader will understand.

At the broadest level, my concern is over the strength and vigor of this sector of our society as compared with the other two, government and business, which have grown so enormously in size and power in recent decades. And, specifically, my concern is over the ability of the private nonprofit sector to play fully and effectively its part in resolving our complex social problems—in helping to bring about orderly change in directions consonant with the Second American Revolution.

These concerns obviously are based on a view that a strong and vigorous nonprofit sector is vitally essential to the proper functioning of an open, democratic, and pluralistic society. To me, a pluralistic system is one in which the door is wide open for options and alternatives to accomplish what needs to be done. Pluralism means a workable balance among government, the marketplace, and individual freedom to take initiatives, with many avenues open within each. There is not total reliance on any one of the three major sectors, but on a functioning and healthy interrelationship among all three.

This diversity and freedom are what basically distinguish the American system (indeed, any open and democratic system) from the stratification of traditional societies and the rigidity and control of the modern totalitarian states. Such systems depend on compliance and conformity. Initiative outside preordained channels is likely to be met with suspicion and possibly repression. In contrast, the American system has encouraged individual freedom and initiative, and in turn depends for its basic viability on response and participation by the individual. Other systems fear free initiative; our system works well *only* when we have it.

The basic strength of openness and pluralism and individual initiative has characterized the United States since the beginning. It greatly intrigued the young Frenchman, Alexis de Tocqueville, when he visited the young nation nearly 150 years ago. His view is perhaps best summed up in the following statement attributed to him:

These Americans are the most peculiar people in the world. In a local community in their country a citizen may conceive of some need which is not being met. What does he do? He goes across the street and discusses it with his neighbor. Then what happens? A committee comes into existence and then the committee begins functioning on behalf of that need, and you won't believe this but it's true. All this is done without reference to any bureaucrat. All of this is done by the private citizens on their own initiative.

The disturbing fact that we must face today, however, is that this individual initiative for the common good, which has been so important throughout our history, is now seriously threatened. As I stressed in the last two chapters, we are now in a period of imbalance, a period when government and business are both extremely powerful, and their power is steadily growing, especially in the case of government. At the same time, the private nonprofit sector has been comparatively weakened. The signs of weakness are real and increasing. There is a shortage of funds and a dangerous cost squeeze for many nonprofit organizations, just when they are most needed. There is a lack of cohesion and sense of direction in the nonprofit field, to the point where there often seems to be a babble of voices, one canceling out the other. Too few leaders in government and business appear to have a genuine and full understanding of the critical importance of a strong private nonprofit sector in the American system.

But I do not want to seem a pessimist, for there are also those heartening signs of new energy in individual initiative I have already discussed—the activities of youth, blacks, women, new "public interest" groups, the consumerism movement, the growing involvement of citizens in political life.

Although it is very difficult to weigh these trends and factors with any degree of precision, I do feel that one conclusion is justified: The great American progressive-humanistic tradition of individual initiative is far from dead, but it is very much in need of understanding, support and strengthening. I would like to devote the rest of this chapter to five of what I believe are the most important considerations in this regard.

1. *The Need for Creativity, Innovation, and Risk-Taking*

Broadly speaking, the private nonprofit sector has always performed two functions: (1) maintaining established and ongoing activities, and (2) pioneering new ways to meet the needs of society.

Clearly, both are vitally important. I would not argue for shifting resources from one function to the other, but for strengthening both. It is simply in the nature of the two functions that innovation will always take a relatively small percentage of available resources, with the bulk going to the maintenance of tested and needed ongoing programs. After all, successful innovation usually results in an ongoing activity which normally requires continuing support.

There is something about the very phrase "individual initiative" which connotes innovation and pioneering to meet new needs. It almost leaps out of the words of Tocqueville. A man sees a need, he discusses it with a neighbor, a committee comes into being, and work begins in order to fulfill that need. How many times throughout our history has that progression of events occurred! The stories of this kind of initiative could fill a whole shelf of books.

In modern times philanthropy has been perhaps the chief institutional means for social pioneering in the private sector. Two good examples in recent years are the fields of population and public television. Both were so sensitive that initial support came solely from philanthropy. The same pioneering function was very much evident earlier in the century in such fields as medical research, educational research, and welfare.

The value of philanthropy as a social instrument was well stated by an especially interesting and authoritative source—the U.S. Treasury Department in its 1965 *Report on Private Foundations:*

> Private philanthropy plays a special and vital role in our society. Beyond providing for areas into which government cannot or should not advance (such as religion), private philanthropic organizations can be uniquely qualified to initiate thought and

action, experiment with new and untried ventures, dissent from prevailing attitudes, and act quickly and flexibly.

It is hard to believe anyone would disagree that creativity and innovation in the private nonprofit sector—whether by individuals, foundations, or other organizations—have been crucially important throughout our history. To me, it is self-evident that these qualities were never more important than now. We face problems of a new and bewildering complexity, and the forces of change are in motion everywhere about us. A key role for philanthropy will be to provide its share of "venture capital" for new problem-solving efforts. Throughout the private nonprofit sector generally, we will need a greatly increased willingness to innovate, to be creative, to take risks, if the humanistic revolution is to succeed.

Perhaps the most articulate and provocative statement of a venturesome role for philanthropy appeared in a book published in 1972—*The Big Foundations* by Waldemar Nielsen, former Ford Foundation executive and president of the African-American Institute. He found the performance of the thirty-three largest foundations in the United States to be generally wanting in terms of innovation and risk-taking. He holds that their mission now should be as "change agents" to help America "through its present agonizing transition," to contribute to "humanizing and advancing American democracy." If they do not rise to this challenge, Nielsen believes, they will become obsolete:

> But if the foundations, particularly the large ones, are judged by the performance of the best of them and if some of their great achievements of the past are kept in mind, it is obvious that private philanthropy has great unrealized potential. This potential is so great and of such special value at this point in American history that it would be reckless imprudence to throw it away.

The wisest course of public policy would appear to be to give them a further chance—for a reasonable but limited period of time—to begin to fulfill their possibilities.

2. *The Need for Increased Financial Resources*

We are well into an unprecedented financial crisis in the private nonprofit sector. Many people have an inkling of the seriousness of the problem when there is a personal tie—to a church or a private college or a valued community service such as a hospital, a library, a museum, a symphony orchestra. But not enough see the urgency of the situation in its full ramifications.

The fact of the matter is that private giving has not increased as fast as the Gross National Product or the Federal budget or the rise in costs of operating. In recent years private giving from all sources has totaled approximately $20 billion each year. In contrast, President Nixon's budget request for fiscal year 1973 was $246 billion. There is perhaps no more graphic illustration of my point about the growing imbalance between the major sectors of our society.

Already we are beginning to see the effects of the cost squeeze —institutions closing their doors or drastically curtailing their services or gradually being taken over by government.

I would like to make it clear that I have nothing in principle against a privately supported organization or function being taken over by government. There are times when this makes good sense. I have spent my life in philanthropy, which is studded with examples of pioneering efforts ultimately assumed by government for such reasons as legitimization or greater scale.

But what does concern me is any massive and seemingly inexorable trend in that direction. When I discussed the role of government in the last chapter, I expressed my belief that such a trend has been operative for a number of years in our society. I see the worsening financial plight of the private nonprofit sector as only accelerating it. The need is to halt the trend and stir the government to take every reasonable measure to strengthen the private nonprofit sector—particularly to improve tax incentives to increase the flow of funds.

Increasing the flow of funds is not the responsibility of the Federal Government alone, however. It is also a matter of individual initiative and commitment. The tax incentives which already exist are not being used to anywhere near the maximum allowed. I made this point earlier in respect to philanthropic giving by corporations. But what is true for corporations is also true for the individual person.

Individuals provide much the greater share of all voluntary giving, more than 70 percent each year, with foundations, corporations, and bequests accounting for the rest. Individual giving has increased every year since adequate data have been available, but in very recent years that increase has not been as great as the increase in after-tax income. Just as in the case of corporations, individual giving varies a great deal—some give until it hurts, while many give scarcely at all. Tax incentives obviously play a very important role, but even more important is understanding the financial threat to private institutions. I cannot stress too strongly the responsibility and opportunity of the individual in this respect.

We need an all-out effort on all these fronts—corporate giving, individual giving, understanding and support by the government. We need such an effort, that is, if we are to have reasonable hope of restoring some semblance of a balance among the sectors of our society, if we wish to preserve and enrich the diversity that has always been so integral to our system.

If we do not make this effort, I fear some future Tocqueville will present us with a very different description of the United States. It will not be a description of a giving society—of the sense of participation and commitment and service that is central to that concept.

3. Self-Renewal Within the Private Nonprofit Sector

The private nonprofit sector needs a great deal of understanding and support from the business and government sectors, but it also must have its own agenda for internal improvements in both of the broad functions of maintenance and innovation. This is the challenge to leadership and management in the field.

When I discussed organizational self-renewal in a previous chapter, the comments were addressed in the main to government and business. But, obviously, the need for self-renewal applies very much to organizations in the nonprofit field, in some respects more so. Far too many of them are "arteriosclerotic," as John Gardner expressed it. Overcautious, they cling to traditional concepts and methods, as rapidly changing times threaten to leave them far behind.

I have spent many years as a trustee of nonprofit organizations, including foundations, and I have followed others closely. I should acknowledge frankly that trustees are frequently the culpable parties when the organization is not creative and forward-looking. Far too many staff members think their first professional objective must be "to stay out of trouble"—not only with the Internal Revenue Service and the press, but also with their own trustees. There is plenty of caution among staff people generally, but to a large extent it is the attitude of trustees which causes an organization to travel the familiar road instead of taking on difficult social problems. One important avenue to self-renewal may be diversifying boards of trustees by attracting more nonestablishment members.

The board is obviously the right body to determine over-all policy and—by sympathy, encouragement, and suitable questions—to aid the staff in applying to day-to-day problems the principles growing out of that policy. And the trustees can play a critical part in encouraging courageous attitudes and hardheaded evaluation.

Internal administration is an important key to organizational self-renewal. I am especially interested in whether staff members feel they have the right to dissent. Do the younger staff members, particularly, feel they can speak out? If they do not have genuine freedom of dissent and debate, then the organization will be seriously weakened with respect to creativity.

I think we need fresh thinking, too, about the perpetuity of programs, and even of organizations. In discussing self-renewal, it may seem odd to speak about terminating organizations, but there often can be a relationship between them. Winding up an organization whose mission is substantially accomplished takes courage and vision, and really may represent the beginning of self-renewal in that resources and the time of people will be released for some new task. This would be a far better way to serve the public interest than perpetuating an organization whose time has passed.

A final point I would make about self-renewal is the need for improved communication within the nonprofit field, more interaction, more cohesion and organization. Of course, many groups—universities, museums, symphony orchestras, and others —do have their own associations. But the nonprofit field as a whole is enormously varied, so that it is difficult to aggregate strength, and communication is inhibited. There is a need for the bringing together of diverse organizations, for providing forums to help nonprofit groups to identify areas of need, trade experience, and further the cause of organizational self-renewal in general.

4. *Business and the Private Nonprofit Sector*

As I have stressed, it is in the best interests of this society to have a nonprofit sector which is strong and healthy. If this is true, then it is clearly also in the best interests of government and business. Most leaders in these sectors certainly have an appreciation of the key role that individual initiative has played in the American system. It is even more important that they appreciate the crucial role it must now play. They must understand the need to keep options and alternatives open, not out of tolerance or nostalgia, but for the long-term self-interest of all of us.

In the preceding section, I discussed ways that the private nonprofit sector could work to revitalize itself. But it needs help. It needs the understanding and support of the powerful government and business sectors. And there is an urgent need for improved communications and collaboration among all three. We need the best efforts of all in an intelligent and supportive relationship.

When I discussed corporate responsibility, I registered my belief that, despite very encouraging beginnings, most corporations have a long way to go in living up fully to their social responsibilities. Clearly, one important means of doing this will be for corporations to increase communication with, and support of, the private nonprofit sector. Building up corporate contributions is critically important, but collaboration between business and the nonprofit sector can and should go much further.

Earlier, I expressed my belief that the spirit of giving must apply not only to resources but also to the giving of one's self—

becoming involved in the solution of the problem at hand rather than taking what often can be the "easy way out" of giving money.

The point was well demonstrated in an effort, with which I have been associated for the past several years, to bring concerned young people and business leaders together to discuss possibilities of joint action on local problems. Such conferences were held in Minneapolis; San Francisco; Jackson, Mississippi; Dayton, Ohio; and other cities. Always the willingness of the business leaders to meet with the young was encouraging—and invariably their understanding of local social problems and appreciation of the concern of the young grew perceptibly. But usually the first reaction was a readiness to give money so that the young people could go to work on the problems. This was certainly welcomed, but the interesting fact is that the groups tended to go beyond that to a realization that collaboration meant more than the providing of funds. It meant the active involvement of the business leaders in working on the problems along with the young people.

With the application of a little imagination, there are many possibilities for business to collaborate with nonprofit groups beyond funding. They could include the commitment of time and energy by executives, the providing of expert help in the form of an accountant or a lawyer or an engineer or a communications specialist, making logistical support available such as telephones, office space, trucks. One possibility is for a company to deliberately and genuinely "adopt" a particular problem or need, as several major corporations have "adopted" black colleges in the South, providing not only funds but expert help and counsel. Other companies have instituted sabbaticals to allow key employees to work for a year on a social problem that interests them.

It is perhaps not necessary to point out that involvement and commitment of this sort not only help in respect to the social problem, but pay dividends for the company as well—in terms of employee morale, attractiveness of the company to new employees, community respect for the company, and the satisfaction and growth that come from participating in something larger than one's immediate self-interest. This last is what a "giving society" is all about.

5. Government and the Private Nonprofit Sector

The need and the objectives to be served by collaborating with the private nonprofit sector are obviously the same for government as they are for business—but the situation is very different.

Collaboration by business is not a formal or legalistic matter, but must be based on understanding and voluntary action. But government has a formal relationship in its power to establish and alter the ground rules—the laws, regulations, restrictions, affecting the flow of funds to, and the range of activities within, the private nonprofit sector. It is in this area—specifically during the hearings in relation to enactment of the Tax Reform Act of 1969—that my concern was aroused over the attitudes and actions of the government.

The Tax Reform Act made some important changes which affect philanthropy directly, and, of course, this in turn affects nonprofit organizations because a great many of them depend heavily on philanthropy for funding.

Ironically, at the very time when philanthropy needs to be strengthened generally, when it should be fully capable of playing its innovative role, and when there should be increased communication and collaboration between philanthropy and government, a number of provisions of the Tax Reform Act work in the opposite directions.

The Act reversed the fifty-two-year trend of encouraging philanthropy. Some aspects of the new law must be welcomed because they help to prevent abuses and misuse of the name of philanthropy. But some unfortunate provisions were included also.

Public criticism of the Act has focused most on the tax on foundation income because of the sheer illogicality of that direct drain on charity. But although this is regrettable, the Act has had even more serious consequences in other areas.

The most harmful provisions, as I see it, are: first, those which discourage new funding for philanthropy; second, those which place what I regard as unreasonable restrictions on the operating programs of foundations; and, third, those which inhibit communications and cooperation with government.

The first, relating to new funding, is basic to the future of the private nonprofit sector and the free play of individual initiative. Obstacles to the setting up of new foundations or to other methods of developing new philanthropic resources can only worsen the financial crisis in the private nonprofit field. Without going into technicalities, one might summarize this aspect of the Act's damage to philanthropy by saying that the limitations on gifts and on the holding of corporate securities will deter the establishment of new foundations or the enlargement of old ones. And, at the same time, terminating the "unlimited charitable deduction" has drastically reduced charitable giving by large individual donors.

Some effort was made to compensate for that damage through certain other provisions, especially the increase to 50 percent deductibility. But in general they were minor factors compared with the sweeping long-term effect of the above provisions in discouraging new philanthropic funding.

As to the second point, relating to foundation programs and operations, the effect has been considerable. At least in short-run terms, the sections of the Act which hamper and restrict foundations in their actual work are perhaps the most damaging features of the 1969 revisions relating to philanthropy. The new rules discourage innovation and risk-taking. Foundations are required to accept "expenditure responsibility" for many grants. The penalties prescribed against the foundations for the mistakes of their grantees are so severe that many foundations are refusing to take any risks at all. There is every incentive for them to "play it safe" all along the line.

In regard to the third point, concerning the relationship between philanthropy and government, the Act's prohibitions against "influencing legislation" and "influencing elections" have an understandable origin. But such rules can be easily interpreted as forbidding anything that by any stretch of imagination might be called "political." There are additional regulations which inhibit communication between foundations and government. That is particularly unfortunate at a time when the need is for better and more frequent contact and exchange of views so the different sectors of our society can work together on our common problems. The relationship between philanthropy and government is, or should be, a two-way street. Many times the pioneering work of philanthropy must result in legislation or other governmental action to be fully effective. And on countless occasions government has found the flexibility and resources of private philanthropy to be invaluable. Never was this cooperation more needed, but the new restrictions have curtailed it.

Fortunately, the Internal Revenue Service for the most part has been interpreting these complex provisions in a broad and reasonable manner. This process of interpretation is still going on as this book goes to press. But the substantive provisions cannot really be changed without new legislation. The negative effect can often be more psychological than strictly legal, for the language of the Act encourages cautious lawyers to advise their philanthropic clients to be very careful. Too many in philanthropy are prone to be overcautious without further encouragement.

One reason the Congress acted in this fashion was a build-up of concern over exploitation of the tax privileges. This was a genuine concern, and responsible people in the field of philanthropy shared it. In my testimony before Congress in 1969, I stressed that "abuses in philanthropy must be eliminated." I elaborated as follows:

> It is . . . essential to make certain that in preventing misconduct we do not endanger the very incentives that make philanthropy possible on a meaningful scale. We are faced with a classic problem: How do we prevent misconduct within a great and needed institution without overreacting to the point where the institution itself is severely crippled? Misconduct must be stopped, but we must not, as the saying goes, throw the baby out with the bath.

I believe that Congress did overreact. The most disturbing aspect was the general lack of understanding and appreciation, within both Congress and the Administration, of the unique force that philanthropy and nonprofit organizations represent in American life. Perhaps the seemingly punitive mood will have proved to be of the moment, and support for philanthropy will re-emerge within government.

However, it is not encouraging to note that more recently several political figures have proposed curtailment of charitable giving in an even more drastic way than that accomplished by the Tax Reform Act. In this extreme view, an "incentive" for giving is seen as a "loophole," which then is regarded as an "abuse."

It is hard for me to believe that any responsible person would want to curtail the financial resources so basic to individual initiative, to creativity and innovation by the private sector for the common good. I wonder how those who espouse such views expect private nonprofit institutions to continue to function— the churches, libraries, museums, hospitals, cultural organizations, social-action groups, and all the rest. The only possible result would be a massive shift of these institutions from private to governmental status, drastically altering the structure and fabric of our society. There would be no financial gain for the government because any additional tax revenues would be more than offset by the need to pay for the support of these institutions. And, this shift from private to public status on such a scale would run directly counter to the decentralization, diversity, and pluralism which are so essential to our hopes of achieving a more humanistic society.

I agree that we need changes in governmental regulations affecting philanthropy, but in precisely the opposite direction—toward removing restrictions on philanthropic activity as well as increasing the incentives for private giving. I believe we need to improve tax incentives for charitable contributions for donors in the lower as well as the higher tax brackets. The desirability of "democratizing" incentives was noted by the Commission on Foundations, Private Giving, and Public Policy—the so-called Peterson Commission, chaired by Peter G. Peterson, currently Secretary of Commerce, which made its report public shortly after the Tax Reform Act was passed.

In thinking along these lines I have been greatly taken with an idea proposed by Alan Pifer, president of the Carnegie Corporation, for equalizing the percentage benefits of charitable deductions of large and small taxpayers. His proposal would allow all taxpayers the same tax deduction as the highest-income persons—a 50 percent tax credit for charitable donations. At present a person whose income is taxed at 14 percent receives only a $14 tax saving for a $100 charitable contribution, while a person with a much higher income, taxed at 50 percent, would receive a $50 tax saving for the same $100 gift. Under Mr. Pifer's plan every donor, whatever his tax bracket, would have a $50 tax saving for a $100 charitable contribution. The virtues of this approach are its simplicity and equity, its opportunity for broader and more democratic participation, and the possibility of increasing the flow of funds to the private nonprofit sector.

I have expressed my deep belief in the fundamental importance of what I have referred to as the private nonprofit sector in American society. And I have discussed five areas in which revitalization of that sector is needed.

If the private nonprofit sector—indeed, our entire society—is to be revitalized, it will be because we, as individual Americans, will it so and make it happen. It will depend on what we are willing to do on our own, what we are willing to do in association with others, what roles we play in the groups and organizations we belong to, how willing we are to extend ourselves beyond our own personal interests. It will depend on our ability to understand that either we must use our freedom to take initiative or we may lose it.

This brings me back to the point at which I started—the concept of a giving society. It is logical to explore this concept in terms of the private nonprofit sector, as I have in this chapter. But it is clear that giving must not be restricted to one sector, but must apply to all of society. It applies to young people fighting for a cause, government servants who are dedicated, businessmen who are farsighted, all those who are willing to lift their sights, both in their daily pursuits and beyond, to work for the common good.

CHAPTER XIV

A Learning Society

THE IDEAL OF A "LEARNING SOCIETY" has been in the minds of men since at least the Golden Age of Greece. That ideal was well expressed by Robert M. Hutchins in his book *The Learning Society*. Such a society, he said, would be

> one that, in addition to offering part-time adult education to every man and woman in every stage of grown-up life, had succeeded in transforming its values in such a way that learning, fulfillment, becoming human, had become its aims and all its institutions were directed to this end. This is what the Athenians did. They did not content themselves with the limited, peripheral effort of providing part-time adult education to everybody at every stage of life. They made their society one designed to bring all its members to the fullest development of their highest powers.

Such a vision bears a direct and obvious relationship to the Second American Revolution. We can maintain a democratic system and move toward a progressively more humanistic society only to the extent that we increasingly have citizens who are alert, intelligent, informed, and involved in the real issues of our time.

The character of a learning society is reflected not only in the formal educational system, but in adult education, access to information, and zealous protection of the freedom of information. Most basically, it rests on the widespread cultivation throughout the society of the realization that learning is a lifelong process, a process that is essential to the full growth of each human being.

The seeds of a learning society were there in the founding of the nation and have continued to exist in the fundamental importance Americans have always placed on education. We recognized early that investment in the education of "commoners" would create the intellectual and technical resources necessary to building a new nation. And we recognized that good government depends on the ability of citizens to understand and evaluate the performance of government.

One need only contrast these concepts with education for an elite, the patronage relationships of the Renaissance, or the Machiavellian strategy of "Keep the populace happy and unknowing," to understand how revolutionary they were.

Formal education is only one element of a learning society, but obviously a key one. The character of a nation's schools says a great deal about the character of the nation. It is in the schools that the society normally expects a major share of the task of preparing its children for adulthood and citizenship will occur. An important part of this process is adaptive—teaching the child to want what the society can provide and to accept the values prevalent at that point in time. At the same time, educational institutions have traditionally served as the breeding ground of new ideas and through them changes in prevailing values and beliefs. The balance between the two forces plays an important role in the rate and direction of change within the society.

It has become popular in recent years to view the educational system as one of our major social problems, and in many respects it is. Yet I submit that what is happening in education symptomizes as much as in any other field the existence of profound currents of change. Education is a faithful mirror image of the society, of its ferment and discontent and quest for something better.

We have seen this clearly, of course, in the field of higher education, in the campus unrest which erupted across the country in the 1960s. In numerous meetings with students and faculty members during that period, I became convinced that to a considerable extent the disturbances arose from a widespread dissatisfaction with many elements of the educational system—the curriculum, the relationships or lack of them among students and faculty and administration, and the very role of the university in contemporary society.

It soon became clear to almost everyone that what was involved was not some passing outburst of youthful energy but real and deeply felt issues, and a genuine desire for fundamental change. Many of our institutions of higher learning have passed through the initial crisis and are addressing themselves to reform and change.

One of the most promising of these changes is the growing involvement of universities in community and public affairs. Academic leaders are realizing that it is a mistake for universities to try to remain aloof and isolated, and that a more active role serves not only the community but the university itself by providing a real-life dimension to the education of students.

Reform has been most visible at the level of higher education, but throughout this same period the forces of change have been perhaps more significant at the primary and secondary levels. Here is where we face directly the question of how we are going to educate everyone, and how we are going to do it well. The problems are pervasive and difficult, as any reader of a daily newspaper knows. Many urban school systems are virtually bankrupt. Ever larger numbers of children seem to be disenchanted with school. Racial imbalances continue. The problem of drug abuse is now much worse in the public schools than in the colleges.

A succession of critics and reformers has given us insights into what is happening within our educational system, which at least partially explain why our schools are in trouble. Among them are:

• Technological innovation and improved facilities do not in themselves guarantee better education.

• What a teacher expects from a child makes a very large difference. If the child is expected to fail, his tendency will be to fail. If he is expected to do well, his tendency will be to do well.

• Lock-step methods and insistence on conformity alienate students and are not necessarily conducive to the learning process.

• People expect too much from the schools. The example parents set for their children, the atmosphere in the home, the impact of the mass media, what children learn from their peers, are all just as important as, and in some cases more so than, what happens in the classroom.

• Children learn at different rates and in different ways. What makes sense in a suburban classroom may not work in rural or urban classrooms.

These insights are not particularly new or surprising. What is disturbing is that the procedures practiced in many schools and classrooms around the country consistently ignore them. It is for this reason, it seems to me, that the current widespread public concern augurs well for the future. The least that can be said is that the situation is very much alive. Not too long ago, our educational systems at all levels seemed to operate in a kind of isolation, which provided an excellent opportunity for stagnation. Professional mystique was strong, and it was a rare parent who would set foot in a school without some feelings of trepidation, a sense of somehow violating some rules just by being there. This is changing now—the doors are swinging open, the mystique is being penetrated, parents are very much in evidence.

All this ferment is a beginning, certainly no cause for contentment as of now. No professional educator, certainly no layman such as I, can examine the range of innovations and proposals that have sprung up around the issues in public education and choose the "right answers." But this should not be a formula for inaction.

Initially we must find ways to ease the financial plight of public education by realizing that it is a national problem of the highest priority. The school systems in about two-thirds of our sixty largest cities are in a state of endemic financial crisis. Some are being forced to close down for one or two weeks or more in order to save money. A number of them are tens of millions of dollars short of needed funds.

There is a growing realization that the present method of financing public education leads to serious inequities. Wealthier communities tend to have better schools than poorer communities. It is becoming increasingly clear that some better method will have to be devised in order to meet the Supreme Court's prescription of equal educational opportunities for all children.

Some have argued for massive amounts of Federal aid as a solution. Others see statewide funding as the answer. While I agree with the need for better and more equitable funding, I think we would be moving in the wrong direction if we let the method we use for meeting that need lessen local control of school administration. In an increasingly self-conscious, pluralistic society we need more diversity, not less, in learning situations. This will best come about if parents have more choices and greater influence over the manner in which educational resources are used.

As important as the financial crisis is, it is becoming increasingly evident that money alone will not solve all our educational problems. After a four-year study of the difficulties confronting the educational system today, journalist and scholar Charles Silberman comes to one basic and clear conclusion in his book *Crisis in the Classroom:*

> . . . the crisis in the classroom is but one aspect of the larger crisis in American society as a whole, a crisis whose resolution is problematical at best. It does no good, however, to throw up our hands at the enormity of the task; we must take hold of it where we can, for the time for failure is long since passed. We will not be able to create and maintain a humane society unless we create and maintain classrooms that are humane.

When I discussed organizational renewal earlier, I mentioned Douglas McGregor and his contention that our theories of industrial management are based on mistaken assumptions about human nature. It appears that the crucial problem Silberman describes derives from some equally faulty assumptions on the part of many parents and teachers: (1) children do not want to learn; (2) if left to their own devices, young people will learn nothing or "wrong" things; and (3) adults, particularly teachers, are the exclusive sources of wisdom. These propositions lead us to conceive of the educational process as being that of an all-knowing adult transmitting knowledge to an unknowing, reluctant child.

The insights and findings referred to earlier suggest an opposite set of propositions: (1) children want very much to learn; (2) given their own initiative, children under proper circumstances will over time learn "right" things relevant to their particular and individual growth; and (3) adults are not always the ultimate source of wisdom.

All three of these propositions, in my opinion, lead toward a pattern of education more consistent with Hutchins' vision of a learning society. If they were applied to the average classroom situation, one could envision a number of fundamental changes. Teachers would be seen less as knowledge transmitters and more as facilitators, creating conditions in which learning takes place. There would be less programmed activity and more room for children to exercise their innate curiosity and individual initiative. The fact that children often learn more from their peers than from their elders would be recognized and encouraged rather than discouraged.

One of the most dramatic new approaches based on these propositions is being tried in the experimental British elementary schools so well described by Featherstone and Silberman and other writers on education. These schools differ markedly from the traditional American classroom. There is no prescribed curriculum. There are no permanent seating arrangements, with rows of students constantly facing the teacher. The day is not broken up into a series of fifty-five-minute segments each devoted to a different subject. Instead, the classroom is divided into a number of learning centers—one having to do with numbers, another with words, another with art. The children in the classroom are encouraged to work in whichever center they wish. The rules are simple—one must not unnecessarily distract others and one must clean up after one is finished.

Observers report that these differences are accompanied by a quite different atmosphere in the classroom. The most immediate is that the children seem to be enjoying themselves. They seem to be absorbed in what they are doing, not bored by it. The norm of the classroom is activity, not trying to find ways to avoid it. Another surprising facet is that the children over time do tend to move from one learning center to another, not hour by hour or perhaps even day by day but eventually and in keeping with their own inclinations. Also, the classroom exhibits a clear sense of community. Children are helping and receiving help from one another rather than competing against one another.

Perhaps the most significant difference in the British experiment has to do with the teacher. While at first glimpse it would appear that the teacher's role is less important than in the traditional classroom, closer observation makes it clear that it is the key to success. In the British system good teachers are constantly aware of the problems and progress of each youngster every day in the school year. The teacher must have the capacity to stimulate the imagination of children and to assist in the development of learning skills based on an intimate knowledge of each child's development and his or her particular and peculiar interests and abilities.

The British experiment is certainly not a panacea. Some children need more structure than it offers, and many teachers lack the special skills needed to make it work. However, the British experience does suggest that an approach emphasizing individual initiative, flexibility, and reciprocal relationships can improve the learning process. These are some of the characteristics that Silberman has in mind when he stresses the need for "humane" classrooms.

Thus far we have been talking primarily about formal educational systems which are mostly concerned with the young. The principal purpose of these systems historically has been preparation for adulthood, which in turn has been seen largely as earning a living, providing a home, and assuming the responsibilities of citizenship. Given this perspective, it is not surprising that "adult education" has been thought of chiefly as compensating for inadequacies in one's previous formal education.

There are signs that the concept of learning in the later years of life is changing and changing rapidly. More and more adults are becoming inquisitive about matters that go well beyond the routines of their daily lives. They are becoming interested in the arts, in nature and the environment, in the society, and perhaps most importantly in themselves as human beings. I can think of no time in our history when the question "Who am I and where am I going?" has received as much popular attention as it has during the last decade. One could cite many examples of this trend—ranging from intense interest in Oriental religions to the popularity of the magazine *Psychology Today*—but possibly none is more dramatic than the growth of the "human potential" movement, which psychologist Carl Rogers has called "the most important social invention of the twentieth century." This approach to learning deals directly with the question of self-awareness through open and free dialogue and personal reactions to individual behavior in small group meetings. I have never participated in one of these meetings, but I am told by others who have that the experience, while at times somewhat unnerving, does produce insights not readily available elsewhere.

What intrigues me about these new directions in adult learning is not the specific subjects or techniques, but rather the shifts in emphasis from the past. It seems clear that many Americans have begun to recognize that learning is a lifetime process that does not cease with a diploma nor necessarily take place in what once was considered an "educational" setting. More importantly, it suggests that many have gone beyond the point where education and learning are seen as merely the acquisition of skills and recorded information. They are seeing that continuing curiosity about the world, the society, their fellow men, and themselves is basic to the development of one's human potential.

Full access to information would certainly be a fundamental characteristic of a learning society. There are two important aspects to consider. One is simply coping with the avalanche of information which seems to increase every year, rather than merely being a passive target for advertising, mass media, direct mail, and all the rest. Although this is a problem primarily in adult life, resolving it is best started within the formal educational system. The need is to help youngsters form the habit of taking initiative and being selective as in the experimental British schools. It is equally important to aid their selectivity by increasing their exposure to a range of information and interests at an early age.

I became involved in such a curriculum-broadening effort some years back. I and others had become concerned over the extremely limited exposure of students to the visual and performing arts in both primary and secondary schools. The result was an experimental "arts in education" program which took the form of several pilot projects in school systems in Missouri and New York. Its objective is to expose all the students to all the arts in the course of their school experience, and to establish the arts as a basic element in the curriculum along with English, mathematics, and science. I believe the projects are proving successful in giving the students a foundation in the arts that will serve them well throughout their lives. They have also provided a model that may be emulated in other school systems.

The second aspect of the access-to-information problem is to be able to find the specific information one wants or needs, whether for special interest or general life enrichment. Modern technological advances will greatly assist, particularly the television tape recorder and cable television systems. They will place in the hands of every person the possibility of learning about any subject which interests him and in such a fashion that the learner will be able to control the process. Interestingly, this implies a turnabout of sorts for electronic technology. It has led us through a mass-produced age of depersonalization, but can now return us to direct and individual communication.

As important as all the foregoing considerations in this chapter are—educational opportunities, learning relationships, access to information—the cornerstone of the learning society I speak of is, and must be, the free flow of information among its members.

Here again our forefathers were provident, for in the First Amendment to the Constitution they guaranteed a free press, knowing that a commitment to mass education would be meaningless unless the populace was kept fully informed on the affairs of state.

Without First Amendment guarantees of freedom of speech and freedom of the press, our ideals would be as empty and hollow as the most extreme critics today claim they are. And, of course, without the First Amendment and the strong tradition it has nurtured, those critics would have a genuine issue—but they would be unable to talk about it.

Today, as in other periods of our history, there are those who feel that the press and other journalistic media have on occasion overstepped their rights, and therefore seek to curtail them. To these critics, I can think of no better response than that made by Thomas Jefferson, who, while believing that his Presidency had been subject to "abuses of freedom of the press . . . carried to a length never before borne by any civilized nation," nevertheless wrote:

> It is so difficult to draw a clear line of separation between abuse and the wholesome use of the press, that as yet we have found it better to trust to the public judgement, rather than the magistrate. And hitherto the public judgement has performed that office with wonderful correctness.

One can scarcely exaggerate the importance of freedom of the press. The United States has the most free and abundant flow of information of any country in the world. It is basic to our strength, and must be zealously protected against those who would remove library books from the shelves, censor films, harass newsmen, place themselves in the position of judging what their fellow citizens can see and hear and learn.

Our founding fathers knew full well the importance of freedom of information, but they could not have foreseen how extensive it would become with the advent of radio, the computer, television, and the explosion of knowledge in all fields of learning. We are deluged with information. The fact that much of it is so specialized and esoteric that it is not readily understood by the mass of people has stirred fears of a "knowledge elite," for increasingly we have become aware that knowledge is a form of power. The abundant flow and power of information have also stirred concern over its quality, as in current debates on pornography, the effect of television and movie violence on the young viewer, and the influence of the press and other media on voters.

The answer to these problems associated with freedom of information cannot lie in restraint or censorship or governmental control of any kind. Any move in that direction is a move away from a learning society and toward a controlled society. Rather than taking this negative path, we must rely on Jefferson's admonition to "trust the public judgement." We must meet the problems with a positive response—by working to improve the quality of information, by upgrading our individual ability to be selective and to discern the truth. This is the path to a society which serves the ends of human growth, a learning society, one in which formal education is humane, learning is regarded as a lifelong responsibility, and the channels of information are forever free and open.

CHAPTER XV

A Planning Society

I HAVE STRESSED SEVERAL TIMES my firm belief that a renascence of individual initiative is the key to success in the humanistic revolution. At the same time, however, it seems self-evident that we need to concern ourselves with new ways to help give order and direction to that involvement. The world has become so complex that growing involvement without a long-term sense of direction may tend to become activity for its own sake. We need to find ways to focus our energy on the best alternatives and choices if we are to achieve the future we desire.

In short, I believe we need to become a planning society, not a planned society. The latter has an air of regimentation about it, which would run counter to the growth in individual initiative I am urging. But a planning society is based on freedom of choice, which requires widespread involvement and maximum knowledge and understanding. In a planned society the plans are drawn and the orders given to the people. In a planning society the people have access to the needed information so that they may participate in the choices that will affect their future.

In speaking of a planning society I am referring to the development of public policy in a way that we have never done before. At present our planning is oriented almost exclusively to obvious problems, with the result that plans are developed on a one-by-one basis. A new plan in one field, say in housing, will be put into effect without systematic consideration of the effect the approach will have in other areas, such as transportation or education or the environment. Similarly, a new plan may be developed by a city without any real knowledge of the intentions of industry or the Federal Government, which will have important effects on the city plan. Beyond this, national policy determination may fail to take account of international forces with a direct influence on our national interests.

A planning society implies a commitment to planning processes on an unprecedented scale, a commitment to the amassing of talent and resources, to the development and use of sophisticated techniques, and to the building of the institutions necessary to carrying out the task. Whenever possible, planning should spell out alternative choices and assess the consequences of each. There should be a continuing effort to relate plans in one problem area to those in other areas. In addition to planning oriented to current problems, a major part of the effort should be concerned with a look at the future of the society. We need to ascertain which of the various possible "futures" is the most attractive to us, and from it to derive plans that will lead us toward that desirable future state. Sophisticated planning should occur not only at the national level, set in the framework of a closely interdependent world, but also at the local level and in the private sector.

If we can build a planning capability of this sort, then it seems to me that we will have a realistic basis for setting national goals and priorities and from them be able to derive programs of action. This approach covers a great deal that is new and difficult, and there is no single term which adequately portrays the concept and its integral parts. For this reason, I will hereafter refer to the concept as "goal-setting," with the understanding that I mean much more than the term itself conveys.

There are understandable reasons why in the past we have never made a commitment to goal-setting on the scale I am proposing here. One is the deep suspicion and mistrust many Americans have had of large-scale governmental or social planning. I can remember only a few decades ago when mere mention of "social planning" would cause the average business executive to stiffen. Partly, I believe, this was a heritage of our frontier experience. With abundance for the taking and room to grow, there was little need for careful and sophisticated planning. Later on, businessmen in particular would equate planning with socialism, with the intellectuals, with the innovations of the Roosevelt era that were designed to pull us out of the Depression. These attitudes have changed drastically, and it has been the business world itself which has led the way in adopting planning techniques, in setting goals, in becoming future-oriented. Quite naturally, this is primarily aimed toward business' own needs, but, by example, if nothing else, it is helping to point us in the right direction.

Another reason why we have not done well in the past in understanding alternatives and setting goals is that we lacked the concepts, methods, and tools to do an adequate job. But this, too, is rapidly changing. There are the advances by the business sector already referred to, which have been undertaken for hardheaded and practical reasons. Academicians have begun to see the need, and there is now talk of a "science of futurism," based not on the crystal ball but on hard, methodical work to lay out alternatives and consequences. Future-oriented institutions have begun to spring up in this country and in Western

Europe. There are developments which I do not pretend to understand—computer models and games, simulation exercises, systems analysis, new conceptual schemes, the ability to handle incredibly large amounts of data in a very short time.

But undoubtedly the main reason we have never committed ourselves to comprehensive goal-setting on a national scale is that we simply did not feel the need to do so. By reason of power, affluence, insularity, room for expansion, native inventiveness, we could always "muddle through" fairly well. Now the situation is changed. Many of the conditions which enabled us to survive and grow in the past either no longer exist or are not as powerful as before, while at the same time the world has become more unsettled and complex.

Many of the major social problems we talk so much about today might have been substantially prevented had we created the means to systematically anticipate where trends and decisions were leading us, and had we gone on from such analyses to establish goals and set priorities so that we could concentrate our resources and efforts. Examples come readily to mind in areas such as urban planning, pollution, transportation, housing, poverty.

Anyone who examines the record will agree that action on a national scale all too often has occurred as a result of self-interest expertly pressed, or as a result of some accident or unanticipated event such as an assassination, the launching of a Sputnik, a prison rebellion, a major oil spillage, a power failure. With rare exceptions (the Marshall Plan comes to mind), we have been reactive rather than generative when it came to charting our own future—responding only when virtually forced to or when problems have become obvious, rather than taking initiative at an earlier stage.

Our approach has not improved even though problems have worsened. Consider, for example, the fact that we know within reasonable limits what our population growth and distribution are likely to be over the coming decades, and that we also know something about the probable pattern of industrial growth in the future. Yet we have no master plan for relating the two, which is essential if we are to have some order in population distribution.

Consider another example. The winding-down of the Vietnam war plus the moderation in defense and aerospace spending have resulted in thousands of highly skilled people losing their jobs. We have functioned as if this were unpredictable. Our reaction has been to develop patchwork programs to help some of these people, but unfortunately we were without a goal, priority, or master plan to make possible the transference of their skills on a meaningful scale to urgent areas of domestic need. Just one of the unhappy results is that we have added strength to the widely held but fallacious belief that a capitalistic economy can operate successfully only if it is fueled by a steady succession of wars. Although this is untrue, we make it *seem* true by our failure to anticipate and plan, by our failure to mount adequate "wars" to overcome our social problems.

Altogether, it seems to me, the evidence is strong that we badly need a new approach to goal-setting. Our problems are growing and becoming more complex. We are drifting into an unplanned and uncertain future. We will no longer have time to "let things work themselves out." In terms of the accelerating pace of change, a month now is equivalent to a year only a decade ago, and equivalent to a decade a century ago. We have arrived at a time in our history when we must learn to manage the forces of change for the sheer sake of survival.

I believe that we are at least at the threshold of developing the conceptual and technical means for accomplishing goal-setting. But actually creating the institutions and processes to bring it about on the national and local levels will be extraordinarily difficult if we are to attempt it in a serious and sustained way, and this is the only way to attempt it. We would be undertaking major innovations—principally goal-setting institutions at the national and local levels—which would have a profound and positive impact on our national life. As Alvin Toffler put it in his thought-provoking book *Future Shock:* "A revolutionary new approach to goal-setting is needed."

The complexities and difficulties involved are perhaps best delineated if I cite what seem to me to be some of the more salient and important characteristics of "a revolutionary new approach" which would effectively serve our need.

Humanistic Rather Than Technocratic

I said earlier that achieving a desirable future state of existence will depend on our ability to synthesize the values of the Industrial Revolution and the American Revolution. Goal-setting institutions should be designed and managed with that process in mind and to become instruments for assisting in its accomplishment.

Goal-setting must be solidly based in humanistic values, and be oriented toward the quality of life—toward achieving a higher plateau of human existence. It must take into account the irrational as well as the rational, the social and psychological dimensions of life as well as the physical and economic.

A humanistic orientation is not only vitally important in its own right for the purposes of our society, but it will also avert an obvious danger. Many of the tools required for successful goal-setting will be very sophisticated, among the higher developments of science and technology. If the technology dominates, goal-setting could become the servant of the technocrats or some elitist group who could use it to increase control over the people "for their own good" in the classic manner of an oligarchy. Therefore the technology must be clearly subordinated to humanistic values.

The Basic Importance of Participation

Goal-setting should be carried out in the spirit of participatory democracy. If a national goal-setting function is allowed to become an isolated "think tank" or if it ends up the servant of any one interest group, the result will probably be worse than our present situation of having no such function at all. It must be the servant of the whole society. Democracy is not a spectator sport; goal-setting must be a dynamic process involving those affected by the goals to be set. This will require that it be open to various shades of opinion, to dissent, to creativity across the nation.

It will also require means for continuous "feedback" to enable testing and evaluation and re-evaluation. It may be argued that present-day America is simply too large to allow for "town hall meetings" or any other form of more than token participation. However, effective use of advances already made in electronic communication and those yet to come could go a long way in this direction. A national goal-setting institution should take the initiative in facilitating participation by reaching out to tap opinion and creativity throughout the society.

But perhaps the most important means of involving citizens will be the establishment of active and dynamic local goal-setting programs. Erik Jonsson, the former Mayor of Dallas, has pioneered in this field by establishing the "Goals for Dallas" program, which embodies an elaborate series of steps to get widespread community involvement. This program has become successful enough to be emulated in a number of other cities, becoming something of a movement in the Southwestern states. Mayor Jonsson believes that the fact that so many citizens of Dallas are involved each year in thinking about the future of their city is even more important than any specific results of the process.

There has been discussion within the Federal Government of supporting local goal-setting programs as a major activity during the Bicentennial era. Many states and cities have shown interest. The approach is particularly advanced in the State of North Carolina, where the Bicentennial program is based on stimulating goal-setting and follow-up action, both statewide and in local communities. Significantly, the program has been entitled "American Revolution II" to evoke the spirit which so characterized the America of two hundred years ago—the resolution to face up to problems and chart the future.

In my judgment, a link between national and local goal-setting is essential if we are to capitalize on the innate strength of democracy. Integrating goals at various levels will certainly be difficult. But national goal-setting without local counterparts will inevitably tend to become elitist. And local goal-setters working without benefit of a national program will be missing crucial pieces of the picture.

Public-Private Cooperation

Early in his tenure, President Nixon created a "National Goals Research Staff" in the White House. This staff was not intended to monopolize a national goal-setting function. Its size and resources were much too limited for that, and members of the staff saw the need for a major goal-setting institution set up independently of the White House, with initiative coming from the private sector. Private efforts to create such an institution have gone through several phases, and are still very much alive. But the "National Goals Research Staff" itself was subsequently disbanded, for reasons that are not entirely clear. This was unfortunate since I believe the pattern envisioned of an "inside" staff and an "outside" institution was a wise one. Yet achieving that pattern may be more realistic, certainly at this juncture, if the private initiative comes first.

The value of this cooperative approach cannot be overstressed. A goal-setting function initiated, operated, and funded by the Federal Government could not be objective, independent, free from constant political pressure. It would become increasingly bureaucratized; it could not successfully and continually reach out to tap areas of dissent. It would be permanently handicapped in dealing with controversial issues and difficult choices. Obviously, the Federal Government must be involved in a national goal-setting institution, but it should not monopolize it or control it.

It seems to me that the situation allows for a very good division of responsibility. Initially, the funding for a national goal-setting institution should come from the private sector, and also the major share of support each year thereafter. The Federal Government should provide seed money and a measure of ongoing support for local goal-setting programs. There will be much less danger of Federal domination if its funding support relates primarily to local programs.

It will be essential to success for there to be mutual respect and effective collaboration between the goal-setting institution and the Administration from the beginning. The funding pattern is important in this regard, but there are other equally important considerations. One is that a "national goals staff" should be reactivated within the White House at the appropriate time for close liaison with the outside institution. The initiative for a major study might come from the White House or a Federal agency or the Senate or the House. There should be strong Federal participation in any working groups set up to pursue major topics since it is difficult to imagine many topics that would not impinge on government interests and responsibilities in some important way.

The relationship would also be conditioned by the reputation which the goal-setting institution builds and the quality of its products. To the extent that the institution commands respect because of its independence and objectivity and quality, its studies often will provide the terms and substance for national debate on important subjects and choices. In this way, the institution will be looked to for authoritative information not only by the informed public, the press, and the academic community, but by government officials at all levels.

Strategic, Not Programmatic

The work performed by a national goal-setting institution should be strategic in nature, not programmatic. Its job should be to identify and anticipate major problem areas, to develop long-term strategies, to relate forces and trends in laying out alternative future patterns. The studies would obviously be future-oriented, some relatively short-term, but others covering a sufficient time span—say, ten to thirty years—to allow for real strategic alternatives.

There would be no limits on subject matter. It could range from specific problem areas to patterns affecting the entire society to important international considerations. But the institution must be highly selective—rather than trying to deal with too many subjects or problems, it must choose those with a high strategic component.

The prevailing view among those who have thought about a

national goal-setting institution is that it should not take a position on any study which it produces. This, of course, is markedly different from the typical Presidential or Congressional commission. The idea is that the main purpose of the institution would be to crystallize alternative approaches to problems and the consequences of each approach, thus presenting the government and the public with informed choices. If the institution is constantly involved in an advocacy role, the fear is that its objectivity and reputation will eventually be compromised. I understand this view, but I also believe that the institution should not be prevented from taking a position on those occasions when that seems particularly appropriate. The institution obviously will have a governing board of the highest quality and standing. I believe that such persons should have the option of expressing their opinion.

It is also vitally important that the institution not be Olympian and detached, but that it constantly be brought back to realism, to considerations of cost and feasibility. For example, it must be well aware that the most difficult aspect of goal-setting often is the allocation of limited resources for the pursuit of a variety of goals. The choice between competing goals is the crux of the matter. Also, it must take into account the search for ways to produce desired results and the perplexing truth that we often do not know how to use resources to yield the social results we seek. An important element of this is assessment. We have been conspicuously weak in evaluating accomplishment and experimental programs.

A Unique Status

From the foregoing, something of a picture of a national goal-setting institution begins to emerge. It would be unique, amounting in some respects to a fourth branch of government, but one without direct authority or power, save the power of knowledge and of the merit and relevancy of its products. It would be free from compromising political constraints, yet its studies and analyses would enter the mainstream of political thinking in the nation. It would have the best full-time staff possible, and a large network of outside participants and consultants.

Obviously, it would be a permanent institution; previous sporadic efforts at goal-setting have failed for many reasons, but chief among them was the one-time character of the efforts. The institution must be so structured and protected that it can deal with the most difficult and controversial issues, so that it can withstand the inevitable "failures" that will occur before conceptual breakthroughs are achieved. A goal-setting function which avoids controversy will be worthless. These are all reasons why support must come largely from the private sector and must be sufficient at the outset so that no one can pull the institution up by the roots to see if it is growing.

The approach I have outlined here is not advanced as any kind of tight and unvarying blueprint. There may be many variations; my purpose has been to underscore the need and what seem to me to be some of the important characteristics.

I do not underestimate the difficulty of creating a national goal-setting institution, nor do I overestimate what it can accomplish. One danger is that the sheer difficulty of the task could cause the concept to be watered down. Can enough leaders in business, government, education, and the foundation world see the need clearly enough to be moved to action despite the difficulties and hazards?

We need to guard against great expectations. A goal-setting capability set up under the best of circumstances is not going to solve our problems. Rather, it is a prerequisite to major problem-solving, an indispensable tool to creating the kind of future we want. Under present circumstances we hide from ourselves most of our options because we limit our vision and our time allowance, because we fail to organize to do the research and reach out for the facts and insights that we need. We must overcome these limitations. We must undertake the task of building the needed goal-setting institutions because the alternative to trying, despite all the difficulties, is simply unacceptable.

CHAPTER XVI

The Politics of Humanism

ALTHOUGH IT NEVER ENTERED MY HEAD during my formative years to think of politics as a career, there has been something of a tradition of public life in my family. My maternal grandfather, Nelson W. Aldrich, was a U.S. Senator from Rhode Island for thirty years (1881–1911), and his son and my uncle Richard Aldrich, was a Congressman from Rhode Island for ten years. In my own generation, my brother Nelsen entered public life as far back as 1940, when he was appointed Coordinator of Inter-American Affairs by President Roosevelt. Subsequently, he became Governor of New York State, and another brother, Winthrop, was elected Governor of Arkansas.

It was therefore not too surprising to me when my son Jay told me that he was going to enter public life in the state he had chosen as home—West Virginia. But there was an element of surprise—and a new direction for my family—when he decided he would do so as a Democrat.

People have often asked me about Jay's decision, whether it disturbed me. It did not at all. I was only concerned that he consider the matter carefully and come to a clear conclusion in his own mind—and that he did.

I applauded Jay's wanting to enter political life for it was another example, one close to home, of a healthy general trend in recent years. I am referring to the increasing interest of many young people in the political processes of our society, and their growing involvement.

Many Americans, myself included, are often ambivalent about politics. Sometimes we see it as corrupt or self-serving, as when we accuse someone of "playing politics." But we also recognize that in a democracy it is the principal process which makes the society work. It is the ultimate vehicle of change in the public interest for the expression and bringing to fruition of the needs and wants of the people.

To the extent that large numbers of citizens become actively involved in politics, the more that political processes will be effective in serving the public interest. To the extent that we disdain politics and use this as an excuse for not becoming involved, we will be helping to bring about exactly what we fear—a politics of greed, corruption, and manipulation, or an authoritarian regime.

If I am correct in the view I have expressed throughout this book, that the people want to see our society move forward in humanistic directions, then clearly we will need to create a "politics of humanism." Our political processes must give expression, coherence, and leadership to the humanistic revolution, and must become the testing ground for the change that will be needed if it is to succeed. A politics of humanism will depend on maximum involvement of the people, on the ability of our political institutions to reflect their wishes as to change, and on the emergence of political leaders who see the vision of a truly humanistic society and dedicate themselves to its attainment.

I believe that a politics of humanism is indeed emerging in

our society today. I am encouraged by the growing involvement in politics, particularly by the moderates, and the increasing evidence that our political system can change.

When I speak of growing involvement, I am of course viewing the political spectrum broadly, which I think is proper. Politics is much more than institutions, processes, candidates, and voting. It covers any activity by the people in which they attempt to influence public policy and the public interest, whether locally, nationally, or internationally. Much of the ferment I discussed in Part One of this book—on the part of blacks, young people, women, consumers—is political in nature. Certainly a peace march, an "Earth Day," an investigation of a regulatory agency by "Nader's Raiders," a "Women's Lib" demonstration, are all political acts. They are not only designed to influence our political processes and institutions, but are supplying some of the humanistic content of the Second American Revolution.

Direct political action has also been growing, in such forms as voter-registration drives, working in campaigns, lobbying, testifying before legislative bodies, running for office. Youth, women, and black candidates are no longer oddities. There is a whole new wave of young black politicians seeking and gaining office at the state and local levels. Young people have become a new source of effective campaign workers.

Political activism is definitely spreading to the large center of American politics—the moderates whom I spoke of earlier as the long-range hope for a successful outcome to the humanistic revolution. This can be seen in such broad coalitions for change as John Gardner's Common Cause organization, in reform efforts within our two major political parties, and in renewed interest in local candidates and issues. City Hall, the county seat, and the State House are not the same any more as this decentralizing trend in American politics begins to have its effects.

Political ferment of the kind I have described has been a marked characteristic of our society in recent years—and is likely to be even more so in the decade of the 1970s. With few exceptions I believe this ferment to be indicative of health and vitality. For this is the way that ideas are tested, issues are raised to visibility, new values are infused—and, ultimately, that change occurs and decisions are made in the public interest.

One of the most hopeful signs is that the new involvement in politics appears to have staying power, which has not always been true of "reform" efforts in the past. The typical pattern in American politics at the state and city level used to be a long toleration of machine rule, and then a burst of energy by reformers to throw the rascals out. But the energy rarely was sustained, and soon the rascals would be back in. Many feared that the growing interest in politics by the young would also be transitory, that if their candidates did not win the young people would conclude that the "system" was hopeless and quit. As long as there are candidates who truly represent their views, it seems clear that young people are ready and willing to be involved.

Staying power is crucial, because political institutions and processes are certainly not easy to change. In *The Greening of America* Charles Reich wrote that the revolution he saw emerging would "change the political structure only as its final act." In some respects, he may be right, but the fact of the matter is that elements of the political structure have changed, and more will change. Moreover, as I have just indicated, the humanistic revolution is inherently political in the broadest sense.

Important and relevant political change can be seen as far back as 1954 in the Supreme Court's school desegregation decision, and even more directly in its historic "one-man, one-vote" decisions in the early 1960s. The reapportionment and redistricting that followed have changed the map of American politics, literally and figuratively. One commentator credits these decisions with "making it possible for the majority to translate interests and desires into politically effective solutions for pollution, suburban sprawl, alienation, desegregation, and poverty."

That most difficult area of change—amending the Constitution—has occurred in the case of the eighteen-year-old vote and seems assured in the case of the Women's Rights Amendment. In an earlier chapter I referred to the reform movement within the Democratic Party designed to make it more democratic and representative. We have come close to improvements in other areas, as in the field of campaign fund-raising and expenditures.

Obviously, the process of change in our political institutions is ever unfinished business. Few would disagree, for example, that our renowned system of "checks and balances" at the Federal level is now out of balance. Most observers are concerned over the increasing power of the Executive Branch. There are members of Congress who would be the first to say that Congress is often immobilized by its outdated processes, of which the archaic seniority system in its committees is only the best-known example. The administration of justice is faltering because of the overloading of the courts. The effectiveness of state legislatures and local governmental units in terms of their increasing responsibilities has become a matter of serious concern. Change is not always an unmixed blessing, however, as indicated in the proliferation of primaries in the Democratic campaigns of 1972.

In speaking about change here, as I have so often in previous chapters, I find this a good juncture for reaffirming what I stated at the beginning: I am not advocating change merely for its own sake, merely to do something differently. I am interested only in purposeful change, change which serves the end objective of a better and more fulfilling life for all.

To make a process of purposeful change effective, it is essential that political leaders emerge who understand and espouse a politics of humanism. I believe this is already happening and will definitely increase in the years ahead. It is almost an inevitable result of the political ferment I have described, and it is indispensable to forming and realizing the agenda for change which the humanistic revolution is all about.

What will be the characteristics of this new leadership?

First will be a genuine concern for the problems confronting this nation and a commitment to getting down to the tough job of working out solutions. Increasingly, candidates who do not have a convincing program for encouraging and facilitating change for this purpose simply will not be elected or re-elected.

Second will be a sensitivity to the political ferment which characterizes our time, a recognition that, more than a "new politics," we have a new involvement in politics, and that it must be responded to, understood, encouraged.

Third will be a tolerance for diversity, a recognition of the inherent strength in differences, and yet a skill in reconciling divergent viewpoints into a concerted whole.

Finally will be a patience that comes from an abiding confidence in our political institutions and the nation they serve, a deep sense of personal commitment to the purposes for which this country was founded.

I have attempted in this book to explore areas of needed change, to help identify the issues which form the agenda for the humanistic revolution. These are the issues which require a politics of humanism, and leaders who embody the qualities on which such a politics must be based.

These leaders are going to have to respond to the people in bringing population and natural resources and the environment into an effective balance on "Spaceship Earth." They will have to help bring about a "humanistic capitalism," to distribute wealth more equitably, to provide meaningful work opportunities, to channel growth more in human than in material directions. Their leadership will be essential in redirecting the role of the Federal Government, in finding effective ways to "privatize" and decentralize, while retaining the central power of rule-setting for the society. It will be largely up to the political leaders of tomorrow to undertake measures to restore the private nonprofit sector to its full capability. It will be these leaders who must have the imagination and sense of mission to support creation of new instruments for understanding alternatives, establishing priorities, and setting goals for the future. In all these ways and more, their participation will be crucial in the attainment of a giving society, a learning society, a planning society.

The relationship between leadership and its constituency is always complex. That relationship was very well expressed by *New York Times* columnist William V. Shannon late in 1972:

> I do not mean to suggest that voluntarism is a romantic alternative to electoral politics and formal government. In a vigorous self-governing society, they are complementary like the left and right hands. If individuals care, then political leaders and government bureaucracies eventually begin to care. Self-government has survived and prospered for nearly two centuries in America because individual citizens had confidence in their own judgment and in their own ability to advance the public interest.

The Second American Revolution requires both people who care and responsive political leaders. Their interaction will be a long-term process which will have its moments of progress and its setbacks. It will not depend upon any single event, not even a Presidential election, but upon the gradual spread of the new values and increasing willingness to face up to our social problems.

The agenda for constructive change is formidable. We confront it at a time when the world is filled with international tension, made terribly dangerous by nuclear weaponry. It is a world with a fundamental and growing imbalance between the "have" and "have-not" nations. I believe that we must meet and surmount our domestic crises if America is to be able to play fully its role of helping to build a more peaceful world, in helping to close the economic gaps. We must make the humanistic revolution work here if there is to be hope that it will work elsewhere in the world.

Can we the people successfully move our society forward in more humanistic directions, toward a higher level of human existence? I believe we have no other real choice. We cannot stand still, muddle through, try to turn the clock back. Any of these courses will not only sacrifice that positive vision of the future, but endanger what we now hold is good and right in our system. Only once before in our history did we face the ultimate test. Now as then, the issue is, in Lincoln's words, whether "government of the people, by the people, for the people, shall not perish from the earth." If it does, there will be no talk of humanism.

And so we confront the ultimate test once again—whether we can crystallize a sense of purpose and summon the will to do what must be done. I believe all the elements are there—in our founding ideals, in the initiative of our people, in the vitality of our society, in the problems we face, in the vision of what we could become. In the last analysis, what happens is up to us as individuals.

PART THREE

A Personal View

CHAPTER XVII

Some Reasons for Optimism

In the course of gathering material for this book, I was privileged to spend an afternoon with Dr. Abraham Maslow, the well-known psychologist and philosopher. It was only a few months before his death. The discussion ranged over many subjects including Maslow's theory of "self-actualization": his view of man ascending a hierarchy of needs, from the basic physical requirements to the higher values, most importantly the full development of his human potential in commitment to something bigger than himself.

Dr. Maslow told me that he was screening himself from current problems and attempting to think about what life could be like a generation from now in a quest for the highest level of development of man and society. He justified this futurist preoccupation with the view that the pressing problems of today will be solved without his help, because the means for solving them are at hand in the form of technology and men of goodwill.

A short time after, I came across quite a different viewpoint in Richard Rovere's article in the *New York Times* entitled "This Slum of a Decade," obviously referring to the 1960s. Rovere cogently analyzed the piling up of crises in our time, our failure to anticipate them adequately, and the ominous strains and disaffections in our society. He questioned whether the democratic experiment could survive this onslaught of problems, and said:

> The decade now ending has been one in which simple intellectual honesty compelled us to face up to the strong possibility that we as humans are just about at the end of our days, that our problems of survival will not be solved because we are simply too human.

I cite these two viewpoints not to criticize them and reject one or the other, but because they offer a beginning for trying to articulate my own thoughts. In fact, I respect both. We badly need men of genius like Dr. Maslow, visionaries who are trying to think through the ideal state of the future. Mr. Rovere is not merely a prophet of doom and gloom, but was trying to portray graphically the seriousness of our situation. Certainly, one approach does project optimism, the other pessimism.

For myself, I am basically optimistic, despite all the awesome problems, and despite all the impediments that we all-too-human humans unwittingly place in the way of effective action. This is an habitual attitude—I am uncomfortable merely phrasing a thought in negative terms. Yet I like to think that my optimism is tempered by a good measure of realism. In the face of the problems I have discussed in this book, only a Pollyanna could be an unwavering optimist. Anyone trying to work on social problems must combine elements of the visionary and the realist. My belief is that it is quite possible to understand fully the gravity of our situation today and yet continue to be basically hopeful and optimistic about the future. I would like to say why I have arrived at this conclusion.

I feel this is an exciting time to be alive. Virtually everything seems to be wide open for change. I look upon this positively for to me it means that everything is wide open for improvement and progress. It means to me that each person has the opportunity to influence the course of events, in however small or large a way. I would much rather be alive during a time of challenge such as this than during a sedate and static period of history.

To face challenges, make difficult choices, overcome problems—these are part of the experience of living, of being a member of the human species. Perfection would be static and stifling. This is why I do not believe in Utopias.

We are alive at a great time in history, perhaps the greatest in all of recorded history, for never were the challenges, problems, and choices more difficult, and the opportunities for human growth greater. It is a time when everything in the situation calls for the intrepid spirit of man at his best. It is a time—and this was not true more than a generation ago—when it is no longer foolish or exaggerated for a person to say: "If we do not make the right choices, we will destroy our world."

It falls upon this generation of mankind, and in a special kind of way upon this generation of Americans, to make the right choices. We have the prospect of attaining not the abyss, but another and higher level of human existence.

There is a parallel here to Maslow's theory of human growth through the scale of values to the highest level. I believe that societies can also attain higher levels of growth in terms of the prevalence of humanistic values, and that as a society we are now in a transitional stage to the next level. There is nothing automatic about the process, but the potential is there.

At a time like this, many feel threatened, believing that such a watershed of change means that the whole world is coming apart. Each person has a choice to make. One choice is to succumb to fear, to feel oneself to be the impotent victim of unknown forces. Another is to withdraw, to try to screen out the world. A third is to see the opportunity for another stage of growth, to become a midwife to the revolution, to try to influence it in positive directions—and in that choice to further develop one's own potential as a human being.

I am optimistic because I see people making the choice to become involved and committed, and I see their numbers growing. I have already discussed the role of the blacks, of youth, of women, the remarkable consumerism movement, the values these movements are projecting, the growing participation of the moderates. I have commented on the spread of humanistic values in education, business, government, and organizational life in general.

What would our prospects be if the enormous problems that exist today were to be confronted only by apathy, despair, ignorance, and fear? How vastly different it is to see these surges of vitality I have referred to, to know that the people, at least substantial numbers of them, are alive and well, determined not to be the pawns of fate but to influence their destiny.

Another reason for my basic optimism is the fundamental strength of our democratic ideals and values, and of a governmental system built upon them. To me, this has everything to do with the responsiveness and vitality I have just referred to above.

In my judgment, the unfolding of two hundred years of the American experience, and in particular the beginnings of responsiveness to present crises, validate what the founding fathers believed but could not prove. It is that democracy is the political philosophy most compatible with human nature, the system that is most flexible and most conducive to humanistic values and human growth.

My experience as chairman of the U.S. Commission on Population Growth and the American Future renewed my faith in the value and effectiveness of participatory democracy. As I indicated earlier, the Commission was truly representative of the American people and there was a spirit of openness among the staff and members as well as in public hearings. All of this meant that much time was "wasted" in discussion and dissent—but what was really happening was a process of interaction, of learning and growing together. In the end we achieved a high degree of consensus, a great deal of mutual respect, and a product, I am convinced, that is very true to the mood and needs of the American public today.

I do not speak of democracy in this way merely for patriotic or ideological reasons. The concern is not whether a democracy is capitalistic or socialistic, whether it is rich or poor, small or large. The only concern is whether it in fact assures access to information, freedom of choice, opportunities for human growth, and other basic human rights.

There is now abundant research to show that an authoritarian system is often more efficient for the accomplishment of specific tasks in the short run than is a democratic system. But the research also shows that a democratic system is more effective in the long run. Moreover, a heavy price can be paid for short-term efficiency in a loss of creativity, a build-up of resentment, a weakening of initiative.

This basic difference in the effectiveness of authoritarian and democratic systems is sharpened by the conditions of change which exist today. Autocracy can work well in a static situation, but democracy works better in a dynamic and changing situation. In a world of constant change, democracy becomes a practical necessity, not just an ideal or a luxury.

This profound truth about the effectiveness of a democratic system is often clouded from our eyes by some of the very characteristics of democracy itself. Authoritarian states appear to be confident and secure and monolithic from the outside, while democracies are characterized by skepticism and doubt and self-criticism. But this is basic to the strength of democracy. It is an essential environment for the truthful inquiry of science. It is only through the clash of minds and wills, through dissent and creativity and human interaction, through the development of options and alternatives, that true progress in human terms can be made. When there is no more dissent, when we cease to doubt and criticize, then it will be time to start really worrying.

I am optimistic because of our extraordinary good fortune in having a firmly rooted democratic system, a system which provides the only conceivable environment for a successful revolution of the twentieth century.

All depends now on how the present generation of Americans uses its good fortune. A democratic system is not some lifeless thing, an edifice, an institution, a museum object. Its lifeblood is the vitality and initiative and understanding and commitment of its members.

CHAPTER XVIII

The True Meaning of Private Initiative

One of the greatest documents in all of human history is the American Declaration of Independence. Its significance lies not alone in what it says but in the act of courage and commitment by the fifty-six men who came together in Philadelphia in 1776, some overcoming doubt and hesitation, others burning with a passion for liberty, all of them finally agreeing that the time had come to state their beliefs and to stand by them.

The Declaration concludes with these words: ". . . we mutually pledge to each other our lives, our fortunes, and our sacred honor." Several of those fifty-six men lost their lives in the struggle for independence and others lost their sons. A surprising number lost their fortunes, some to the point of destitution. But not one lost his sacred honor.

Often, it is difficult to identify with actions taken so long ago. The founding fathers seem to be either larger than life or the figures of romantic legend. But the stark fact comes through: the men who created and signed the Declaration of Independence took an enormous risk. They performed a rare act of courage, placing their sense of what was right over their personal comfort and security. And many thousands of other Americans, ordinary, everyday people, also took that risk and faced a bleak and uncertain future and persevered until the struggle was over.

Now that we are well into the era of the American Bicentennial we can expect plenty of Fourth of July oratory calling upon us to rekindle the "Spirit of '76," to emulate the courage and vision of our forefathers as we try to deal with the problems of today's world. That would perhaps be easier to do if the situation of today were more similar to that of two hundred years ago. We face a range of complex social problems rather than the single great objective of winning political independence. Today's revolution is open-ended; it will not be marked by some finite point of accomplishment such as the end of a war. We are confronted by global issues, not a struggle in one isolated corner of the globe.

Yet, even as one tries to articulate the differences, the underlying and profound similarities begin to come clear. The actions of two hundred years ago may have been isolated geographically, but the principles and ideals involved were universal. Today, just as then, we are in a time of profound social change involving masses of people. We are dealing with the very root and structure of society. The first American Revolution did not occur on July 4, 1776, or even in the year 1776, but worked out its full course over a period of several decades. That will be just as true of the Second American Revolution.

Our need today is to summon within ourselves the energy and wisdom to influence our destiny just as our forefathers did two hundred years ago. This is what the Bicentennial should be all about, not just festivities or a review of the past. I have nothing against fireworks and parades. And I believe the renewed interest in our history is extremely important. But I submit that the ultimate test of our vitality and spirit will be the extent to which we come to grips with today's problems and the setting of goals for the future, just as the founding fathers did in their time. The Bicentennial will be meaningful and productive if it becomes an era during which the power of private initiative is rediscovered.

I know that to many people the term "private initiative" has come to be synonymous with *laissez-faire* economics, a kind of businessman's code word for a minimum of government regulation. This is unfortunate, and I would like to see the term restored to its original meaning: free men and women making free choices—that was the "Spirit of '76," and it was the spirit which Tocqueville marveled over and described so well.

I should make it clear that when I speak of private initiative in this way I do not mean selfish individuality. I mean individual action taken for the benefit of the community, for the common good. Private initiative of this caliber is essential to the maintenance of a sound democratic system and social progress. There is nothing automatic about democracy. There will always be authoritarians ready to take over when a democratic system loses its vitality and competence. In the very nature of a democratic system, vitality and competence can come only from widespread commitment and involvement by its members.

In earlier chapters I tried to deal with a number of major problem areas, and where possible I attempted to express my own opinion about what could or should be done. In virtually every case I find that the major problems of today all ultimately come down to one indivisible truth. That truth is that no problem can be solved or dealt with adequately without the understanding and commitment and involvement of people, individually and in groups.

I do not mean to minimize the role of leadership. It is critically important. But in a democratic system leadership must earn its way. It must interact with the people, earn its response, meet the ultimate test of the public judgment—or step aside. The revolutionaries of two hundred years ago could not be defeated because the cause existed not only in the hearts and minds of the fifty-six signers of the Declaration of Independence but in the hearts and minds of hundreds of thousands of people now nameless to history, but powerful because they were moved to action individually and on their own conviction.

That same power exists today, and there are growing signs of its being mobilized. In many areas it is latent. There is no problem facing us that cannot be solved if sufficient numbers among us take the time to try to understand it, to get involved. There is a saying, attributed variously to the Seabees in World War II and to VISTA, which captures the essence of this truth: "If you're not part of the solution, you're part of the problem." To me this is a quite profound statement.

The essence of private initiative is the decision by individuals to become involved and committed to something larger than themselves. It is their deliberate determination to put aside the temptations, distractions, and pressures for conformity which press in on all of us in our everyday lives. It is their belief that the moral and ethical transcend the selfish and the material. And it is having the courage to take actions based on those beliefs.

Most basically of all, it is the realization of individuals that they alone can make the decision to become involved, and that if they do not they may miss their most important chance to feel a sense of inner power, to become whole human beings. Dr. Maslow has stated this ultimate human responsibility very well:

We should now consider ourselves self-evolvers. This is a new age, a new era in the history of mankind, because now we can decide ourselves what we are to become. It was not nature or evolution or anything that would decide. We must decide, and we must evolve ourselves, shape ourselves, grow ourselves; we must be conscious of our goals, values, ethics, and the direction we want to go.

Many people who want to become involved are stopped by the age-old question: As an individual, what can I do, or what should I do? Many people are defeated by the view that their vote does not really count or that their involvement in a cause or an activity really will not make enough difference to warrant the effort. Some feel that the problems are so big and complex that nothing they can do at their level can contribute to a solution.

But the decision to get involved by each individual person may be more important than any measure of how productive or influential one's actions ultimately may be. There is a subtle truth imbedded here which relates what I am trying to say back to the discussion of democracy in the previous chapter. It is that the *way* something is done, the *process* by which it is done, is just as important as the goal or task that one has chosen to accomplish. Think of how familiar a term "democratic process" is. The basic process of a democracy is the free choice by its citizens to become involved in the work of the society in meeting its needs. The small step of the individual person of becoming involved is the beginning of a process. Through many such small steps, understanding develops, consensus is built, and, ultimately, large problems are resolved.

Most people have to start with small personal decisions, to look around their communities and see what the needs are. In the manner of Tocqueville, they might walk across the street to consult a neighbor, and end up forming a committee. Another person might see that the greatest need for his personal involvement lies within his own family. Still another, a government employee perhaps, might see that his best opportunity for constructive influence is within his own agency, to work to make it more responsive. Similarly, a businessman who realizes that there are needs within his company just as important as productivity and profits might move to implement them. Others might find within themselves the capability to be influential on the scale of a Ralph Nader or a John Gardner.

I believe that democratic processes in our society have as much vitality now as at any period in our history. Increasing numbers of people are rediscovering private initiative, learning anew its true meaning. This is leading us to many more alternatives for action and the solution of problems than before. It is building awareness of the extraordinary importance in a democratic system of process and alternatives, of how sharply these characteristics differentiate democracy from other systems. Most basically of all, we are rediscovering that private initiative *is* democracy in action.

Will this process of involvement continue to grow and broaden, and will it in the main be directed toward humanistic ends? This can only be answered on faith. For my part, give me the decision to become involved by more and more people, and I will gladly take my chances as to the quality of their choices and actions. In his own eloquent way, the late Whitney Young expressed his faith:

> I do have faith in America—not so much in a sudden upsurge of morality nor in a new surge toward a greater patriotism—but I believe in the intrinsic intelligence of Americans and of the business community. I do not believe that we forever need to be confronted by tragedy or crises in order to act. I believe that the evidence is clear. I believe that we as a people will not wait to be embarrassed or pushed by events, into a posture of decency. I believe that America has the strength to do what is right because it is right. I am convinced that given a kind of collective wisdom and sensitivity, Americans today can be persuaded to act crea-

tively and imaginatively to make democracy work. This is my hope, this is my dream, this is my faith.

I have the same faith in America, in the countless numbers of men and women of goodwill in our society, those who should see and understand and act. The people are still capable of controlling their destiny.

CHAPTER XIX

The Quality of Life

THIS BOOK HAS RANGED over a number of subjects, but the basic concern throughout has been the broad currents of social change now prevalent in the United States and in the world. I have tried to interpret the profound shifts in values now going on, to understand the issues at stake, and to see ways to influence social change in positive directions. I have said that the goal of the Second American Revolution is to achieve a humanistic society—one in which there is full and genuine opportunity for the "quality of life" to become a reality for all persons.

Now as a final word, almost a postscript as it were, I would like to say what the "quality of life" means to me personally.

It is a phrase much used of late, in speeches by national leaders and in ordinary, everyday conversation. I have noticed that President Nixon several times has interpreted the "quality of life" as the modern counterpart to Jefferson's immortal phrase "the pursuit of happiness." The growing attention now being given to the qualitative is one more proof to me that material progress by itself does not create the good life. In the

United States and other developed societies there has been such concentration on material progress that we have all but neglected our human and environmental problems. Now we are increasingly concerned with what life is all about.

The more I have thought about the quality of life, the more I have realized how infinite and complex the subject really is, how much each man and woman must decide for themselves what it is that gives life meaning. There is no precise definition that can be applied to all people everywhere—but I believe most of us would agree that there are some universal characteristics or elements.

Certainly one is that there can be little hope for the higher values that give life quality unless the basic physical necessities are provided for. Without the minimum needs of food, clothing, and shelter, any discussion of the quality of life is essentially irrelevant. Many centuries ago, the Roman statesman Cato made the point very simply: "It is a hard matter, my fellow citizens, to argue with the belly, since it has no ears." The physical level of existence also includes the relationship of man to his natural environment. Subsistence today means more than food, clothing, and shelter. It also means clean air to breathe and clean water to drink.

It is at this level that we begin to distinguish man from animal, to come to the specifically human values that make life worth living. The Biblical source of the familiar old saying, "Man does not live by bread alone," reminds us that it is a subject that is far from new. There are so many ways to consider it, so many values to discuss and choices to make, in the constant and wonderful variety of human experience. Any attempt to reduce this to some formula or list is to some extent artificial, and yet useful, I believe, as a guide to personal thought and action. For myself, there are five elements which I consider fundamental to a life of quality.

First on my list is *human dignity*. I see this both as an individual quality and a social value. It is a reflection of the individual's relationship with himself, of the degree to which he possesses self-respect, self-confidence, and self-reliance. It is also a quality of empathy, of the ability to identify with other human beings and understand their problems, fears, and needs. Dignity cannot be attained by disrespect or intolerance for other persons. When a man attempts to relegate another man to a lower status, he only displays his own insecurities.

Dignity is born out of a recognition that each of us has unique qualities and that each of us has something of value to contribute to other human beings. As such, it is the foundation for a humanistic society.

The second element which stands out to me is that of *belonging*. As the material side of life is concerned with man and his physical environment, so the higher values encompass man and his social environment.

In the memorable words of the poet John Donne, "No man is an island, entire of itself." Man is, instinctively, a social animal. He has always created social units such as the family, the tribe, the city, and the nation-state. The specific condition of man is belonging, not alienation. There is security in being part of a larger group. The individual can rely on others to help him along in difficult times, and the security of the group can strengthen his inner resources. Further, the individual has the opportunity to be of service to other human beings and thus feel that his life has a broader meaning.

There can be no human dignity, no sense of worthwhileness, when man is alone in a Hobbesian jungle. Our allegiance is not to an all-powerful state or to a selfish individuality, but to ourselves and to others in a balanced relationship—knowing others, supporting others, and finding support in return.

The third element I want to speak of is *caring*, a value which has an obvious close relationship to belonging. There can be no sense of belonging without caring, without a deep commitment to the essential humanity and worthwhileness of oneself and others.

Caring is an implicit, if not explicit, precept of almost all the great religions of the world. It is a quality which has made some of the great leaders of this century especially memorable, men like Magsaysay of the Philippines and Gandhi of India. Many years ago I remember a friend telling of seeing photographs of Franklin D. Roosevelt in the homes of Latin-American peasants. When he asked the reason for this, he was told they believed President Roosevelt cared about them and their problems.

It is quality not only for great men but for everyone. It is giving of oneself.

The fourth element is the need for each person to work toward attaining his *full potential* as a human being. To me, this is virtually synonymous with the idea of a life of quality—it is the specific human responsibility of each person to develop his powers and talents to the maximum extent possible.

This requires both individual initiative and conditions within the society that favor self-development. In any society there is a tremendous range of opportunities to be of service. Too often we are blind to them or do not see ourselves as relevant. As I said earlier, there is too much of a tendency to think that only government can be effective in dealing with the problems around us. There is great power to be unleashed in applying individual initiative to community needs—and no more rewarding way of developing one's full capabilities as a human being.

Much depends on the extent to which the society is an open one. If a person is held back because of sex or race or social position or political beliefs, then perhaps his or her initiative and talent will be underutilized. It is tragic how human resources can be wasted in this way. Even in societies that are relatively open in a political sense there can be strong pressures for conformity. In this situation the most important role for private initiative is to work for change in the society—to bring about openness and opportunities for human growth.

Finally, one cannot talk very seriously about the quality of life without a fifth element—*beauty,* a sense of the aesthetic. It might seem logical to say that we must work on the big problems of the world first—war, racism, poverty, population—and only then will there be time to worry about the aesthetic values of life. But what will it profit us if we do solve the great problems and neglect and lose our sense of beauty in the process? We need this if we are to be whole human beings. Without a sense of the aesthetic we become immune to ugliness and blight. Ugliness is depressing to the spirit and the intellect; beauty awakens them both. In so many ways, it provides the key to the higher values—to the understanding of ourselves, to the enrichment of our individual lives.

Clearly, not everyone can be a great artist or a creator of beauty, but each one of us can develop a keener appreciation of the aesthetic. We should strive to support and encourage those among us who do possess creative talent and can enrich the lives of all of us. And we can find beauty in small things, in our own surroundings. We can find it in our own lives and human relationships, and in a oneness with nature, a new and harmonious relationship with our natural environment.

These, then, are the five elements that stand out in my mind as I think about the quality of life. You may well have others that you would substitute or add. What counts perhaps is not the specific values, but the recognition by all of us that we need to reach beyond the material and concern ourselves with what makes life really worth living—and loving.

Index

185

DA